D0329039

OPTICAL ILLUSIONS
&
PICTURE PUZZLES

Also in this series:

Mind Benders: Adventures in Lateral Thinking
by David J. Bodycombe

By the same author:

The Mammoth Puzzle Carnival

The I.Q. Obstacle Course

The I.Q. Mine Field

Devised by

David J. Bodycombe

With an introduction by

Victor Serebriakoff

Hon. President of International MENSA

This edition published by Barnes & Noble, Inc.,
by arrangement with Robinson Publishing

The use of copyright clipart originated by Corel Corporation, Techpool Studios Inc., One Mile Up Inc., and Image Club Graphics Inc., is acknowledged.

1999 Barnes & Noble Books

ISBN 0 7607 1255 7

Printed and bound in Singapore

02 03 M 9 8 7 6 5 4

INTRODUCTION

By Victor Serebriakoff,
Hon. President of International MENSA

David Bodycombe and I are incurable mystifiers. Not for us the simple mind-stretcher that can be solved in a minute or two. Our puzzles are full of unpredictable twists and turns designed to screw and wring your mind to breaking point.

This book of picture and graphic puzzles descends to new depths of deceit and deviousness. Only the stout-hearted puzzle addict is likely to stay a course so well scattered with minefields and secret traps as David has laid out here. Pause dear, cherished puzzlist before you dare to enter the uncharted dangerous ground. You have been warned. The notice is clear and plain: *Dangers Ahead*.

Graphical and picture puzzles have a special problem. Other types of puzzle are simplified by the fact that they come to you as a string of symbols, words, letters or numbers. To get your mind around a graphic puzzle, it has to be comprehended as a whole. Further, we are not limited to casting the puzzle in terms of simple, known objects and precepts. Instead, all sorts of new and unfamiliar combinations of shapes and forms in the full spectrum of shades add to the confusion.

With the limited range of standard letter and number symbols (just thirty-six of them!), you have a better chance than you do here – when the mischievous setter is free as a bird to invent a virtual infinity of odd and peculiar forms with which to confuse and distress you.

I can only inform and warn. You have about two hundred million receptor cells in each of your eyes. They all play a part in informing you of what is to be learned from each of the picture puzzles here. You have, in effect, to receive and deal with that vast number of constantly changing inputs or afferent signals several times a second to make sense of what you see.

You learned to make sense of the constant information bombardment as a baby, but as you grow older your ability to understand new patterns declines. You long ago learned a large vocabulary of words, and it's not often that you see one you do not know. Even when you do, its meaning is usually quite clear from the context. But, with the vast number of complex new designs that can now be created with the help of a modern computer, the balance swings towards the setter and against the solver.

I know this game very well. After service in World War Two, I found myself in the wood trade and was beset by the problem of grading timber for structural and decorative use. As an inventor I began to think about the computer as a way to do automatic grading or quality control. It was when I began to write programs that I came up against the vast problem of interpreting a visual input. In learning to recognize the simplest shape you have to know about both shape itself and its variability.

So, and this is the last warning, have a care what you are at when you open this apparently harmless and attractive little book. It will have not a few disturbing surprises for you. On the other hand, there is more joy in the "Eureka!" moments you will get when the puzzle suddenly unravels itself and you see through the fog of mystification.

So take courage, have a care, and yes, have a go.

How many circles can be drawn so that the perimeter of each passes through the exact middle of one red, one blue and one yellow star?

One correct circle has already been drawn to give you the right idea, and every circle you draw must fit on the page.

Which four of these six pieces can be used to form the famous "two faces making a vase" illusion?

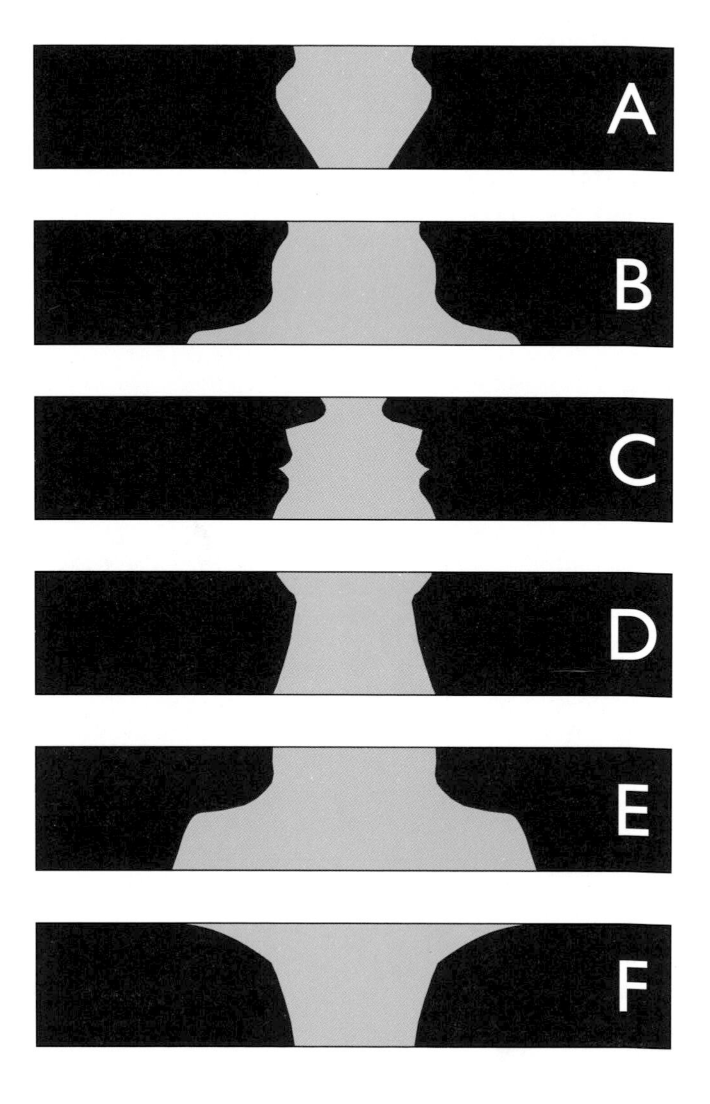

Here are ten of the first eleven letters of the alphabet.

By finding the right sequence, it is possible to spell out an eight-letter word without using any letter more than once.

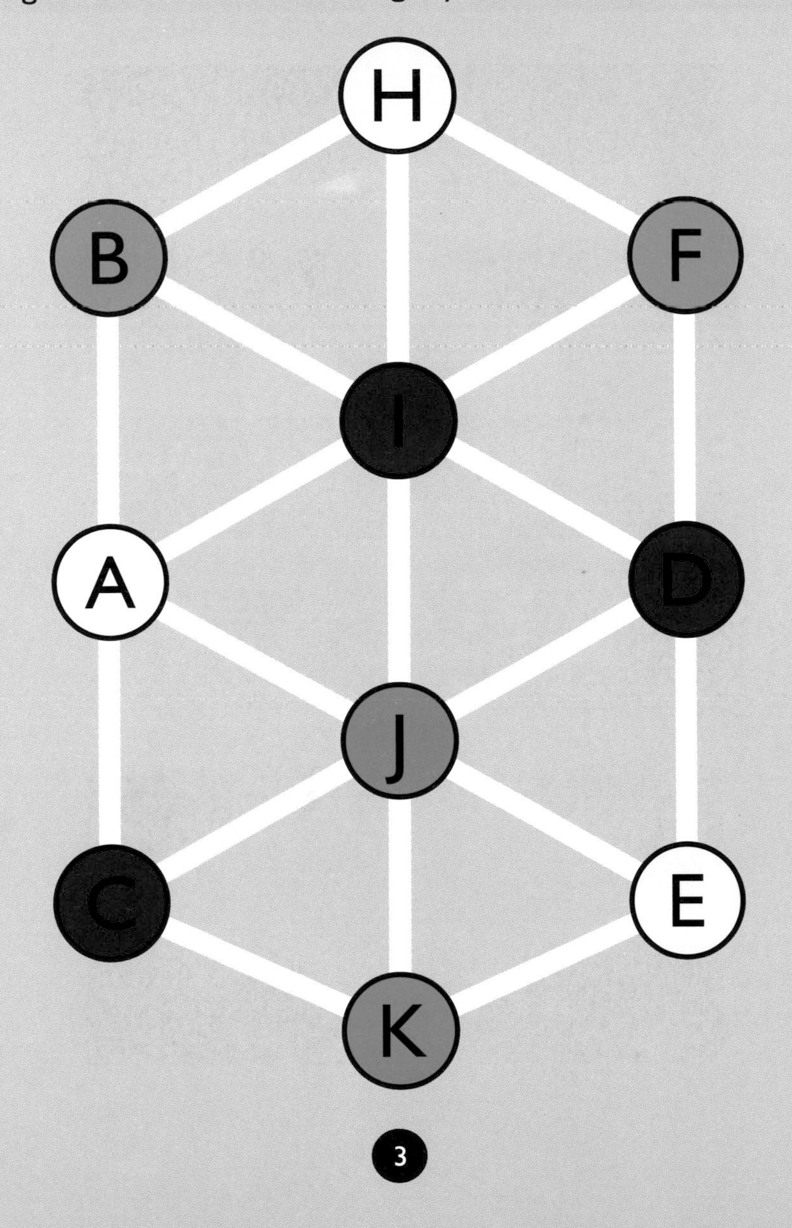

Deduce where the seven values on this wheel of fortune should go. The three clues given might not seem like enough information, but with some lateral thought it is possible.

Also note the direction of the arrows of the wheel.

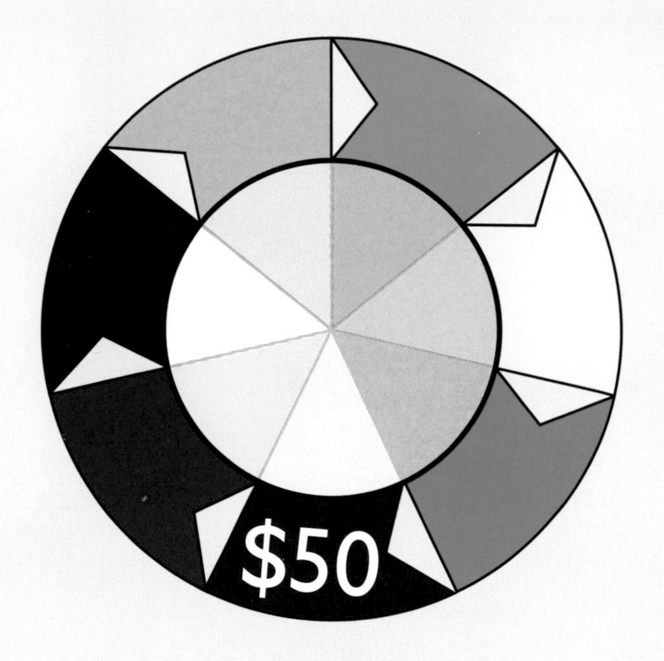

CLUE 1. $25 is four spaces after the $10 win.

CLUE 2. The $100 prize appears between the lousy $1 and $2 payouts, in some order.

CLUE 3. The $5 position is three spaces after the $1.

In this maze, you are trying to reach the finish marked "F".

In the diagram, the number in each cell represents the number of **straight line** moves you must make on your next move.

As you start on the 3 at the top-left, your only two possible starting moves are as shown.

Can you see a simple route through the maze?

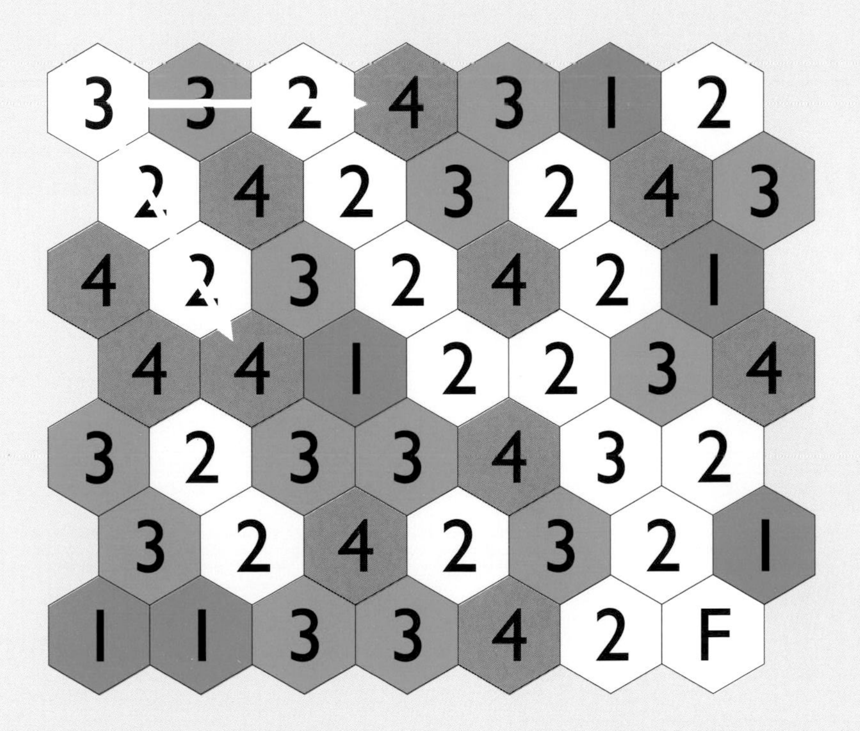

This is one of the simplest optical illusions known. Where is the front of this box?

Either way, here's a further challenge. As it stands, this figure is impossible to trace with a pencil without taking the pencil off the page or using any line twice.

How many lines do you need to remove so that it becomes possible to draw the figure according to these rules?

When I pull both ends of the rope in the direction illustrated, I find that the rope doesn't form any knots. Furthermore, the rope snags one of the nails.

Which nail?

Simply determine the number of targets that are illustrated here. Assume that you can see at least part of every target.

This optical illusion is made up of several impossible triangles.

Imagine that the illusion is possible to make out of box metal tubing. Further suppose we put the cube shown inside the figure as shown (with blue side uppermost) and then send it on an entire "circuit" around the tube.

What side will be uppermost on its return?

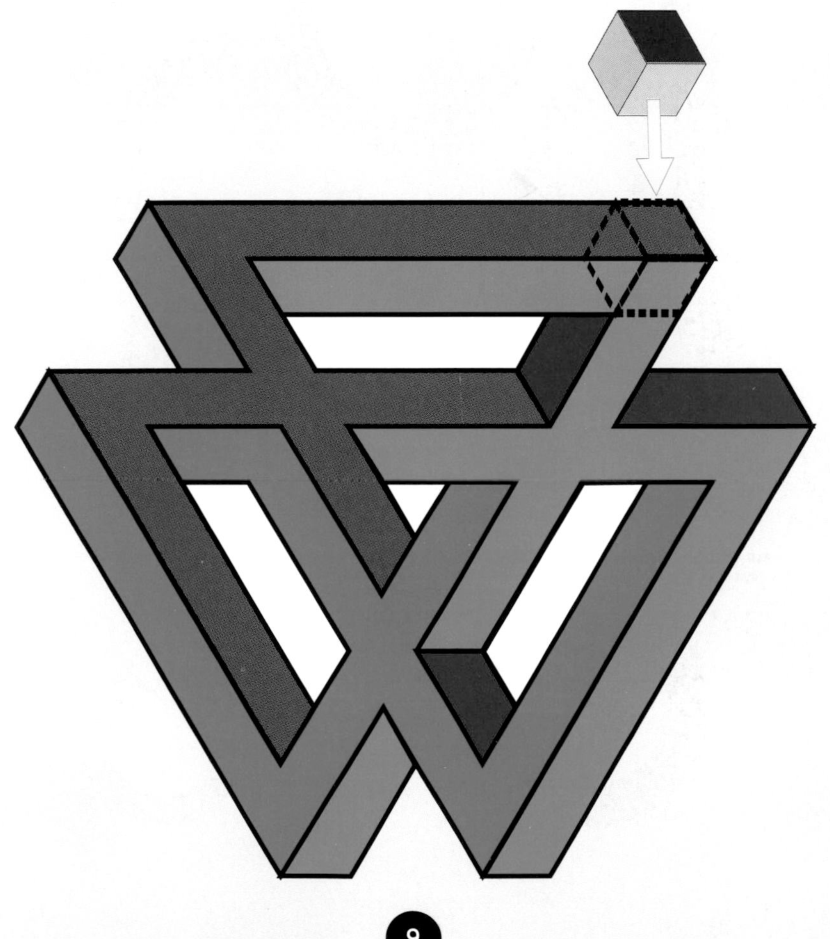

The sides of this square are perfectly straight – use a ruler to check if you don't believe me.

A puzzle for the mathematically minded: If I redrew this diagram using 100 circles (of radii 1, 2, 3, ..., 99, 100 units) and a square with diagonals 200 units long, how many circles would ***not*** be cut by the sides of the square?

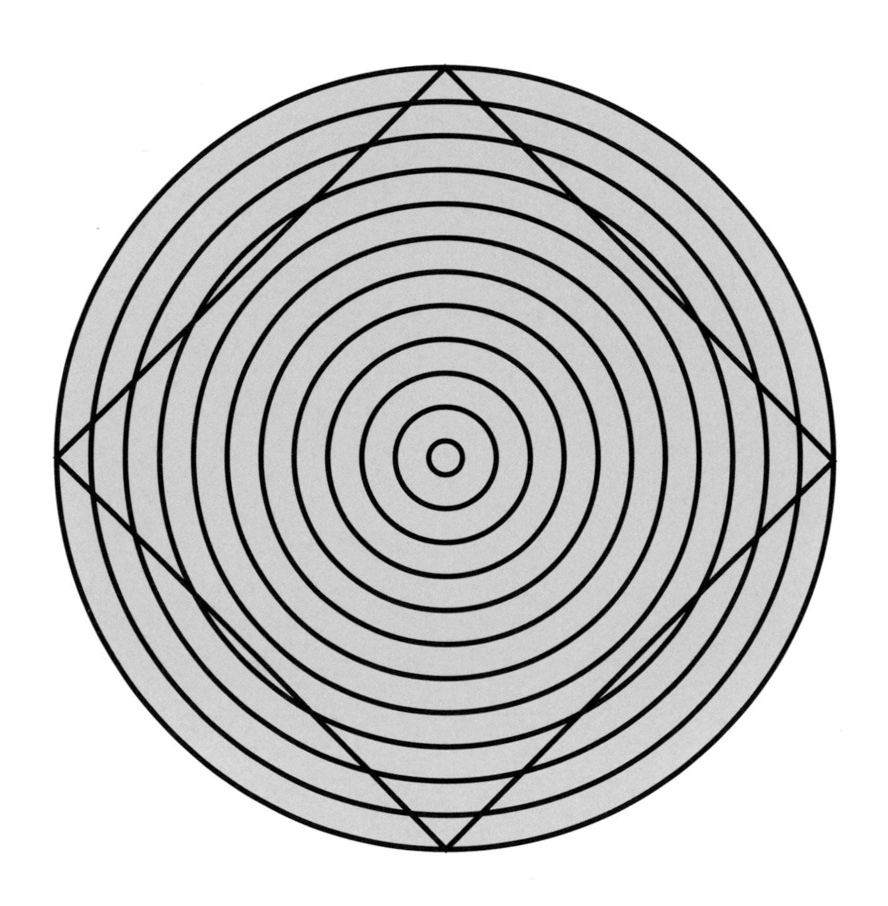

Here are 20 matches, four in each of five types.

Move all four of the matches in two of the five shades to make thirty squares.

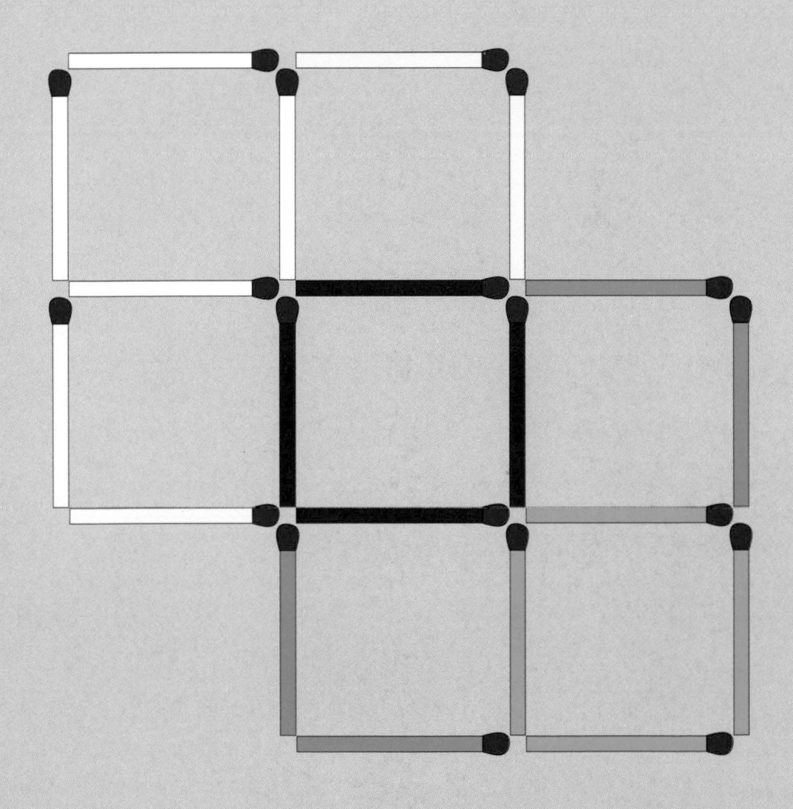

In this illusion, your task is to determine which dot marks the triangle's center of gravity.

And which dot is half-way up the total height of the triangle?

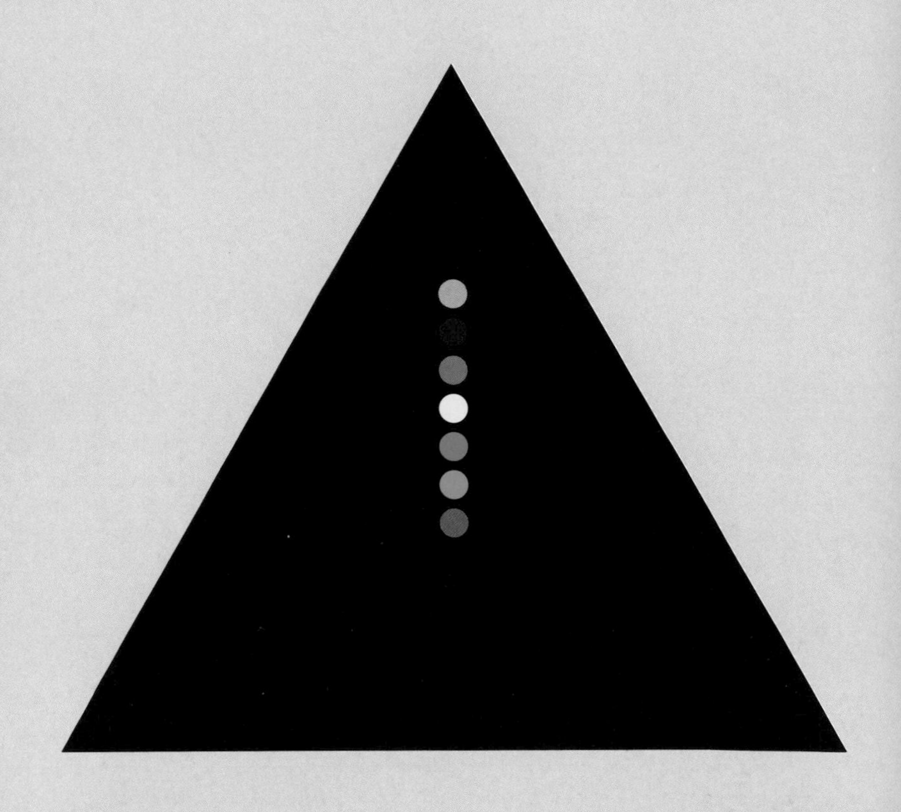

Which star does not belong in this constellation?

Here's a puzzle I know you'll get right.

Which is the odd one out?

Here's an illusion I discovered by accident when designing the graphics for another puzzle. A set of blue concentric circles have been overlaid on an identical set of red circles but displaced slightly. Ten lighter radial lines can clearly be seen. (If not, look at the book at arm's length.)

What will happen to the number of radial lines if I move the sets of circles a little *further apart*?

Suppose you were in this maze for real, and you couldn't tell where you were. At each T-juction you choose your next direction at random, but *you never choose to go back the way you came*. You lose if you use any part of the maze twice. You win if you reach the Finish without losing.

What would the probability be of you beating the maze?

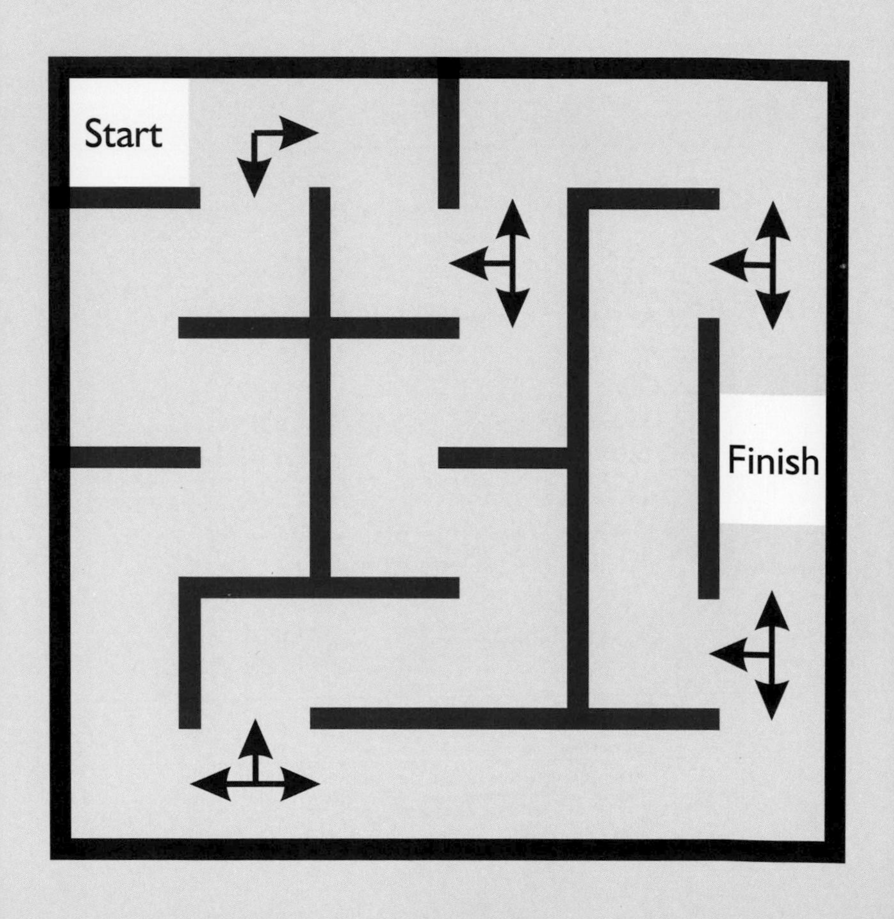

Build yourself a rocket to find the answer.

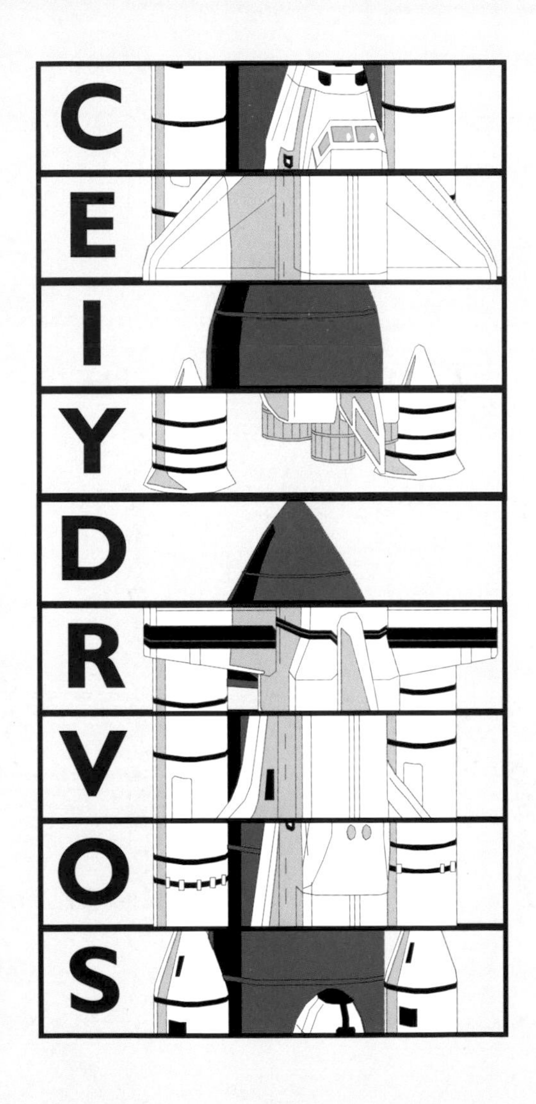

On a roulette table, a variety of possible bets can be placed by any one player. You can bet on the winning number being red or black, odd or even, or in the range 1–18 or 19–36. Each of these bets pay even money (i.e. if you win, you get the same amount back + your bet returned).

Also, you can bet on the ranges 1–12, 13–24 or 25–36, or the three different "columns" on the table. These bets pay odds of 2–1 (double your money back + bet returned). The diagram explains all the other possible bets available.

Suppose I place a $1 chip on **every possible bet** that will pay out if 17 wins. If 17 really does come up next, what would my winnings be?

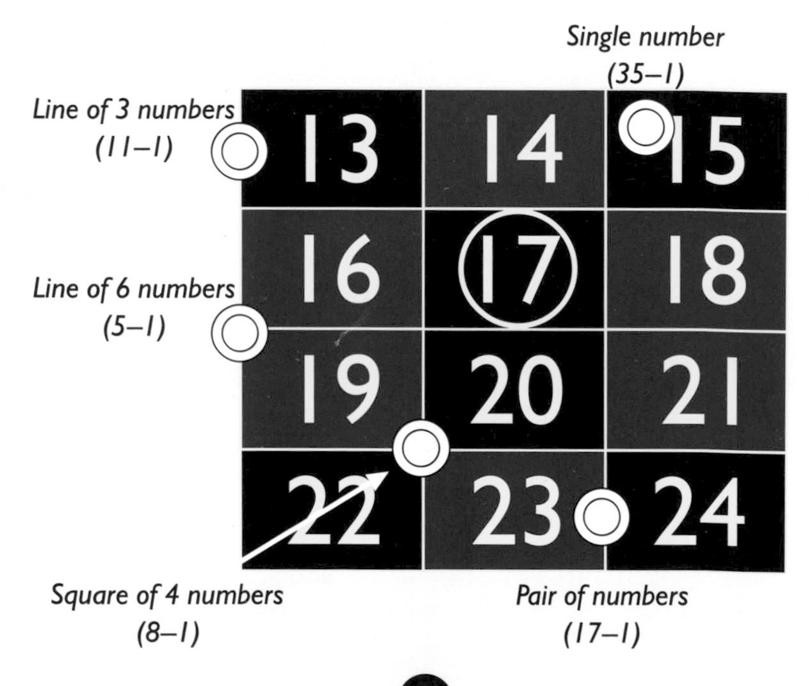

The patterns on this compass make it look three-dimensional.

Also, the letters on the compass look strange. However, it is not a mistake and there is a good reason for this.

What is that reason?

It was meant to be the Olympic symbol, but unfortunately I think I've messed it up. In fact, I feel certain that:

1) Every ring is in completely the wrong place.

2) I've even got all the links wrong (for example, I know yellow doesn't link with red or green in the real picture).

3) I'm sure the black ring is somewhere on the top row.

This is just enough information for you to *logically deduce*, without too much effort, the correct Olympic symbol.

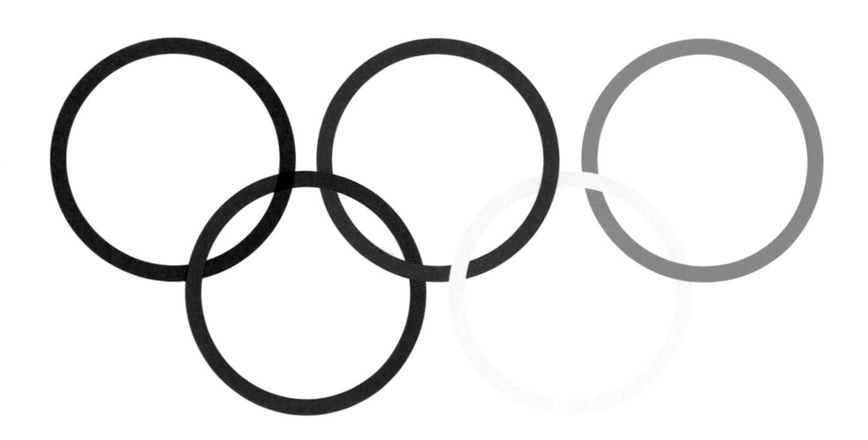

Which one is missing?

Look carefully at these shapes. Rearrange them into an optical illusion that will tell you where to find the treasure.

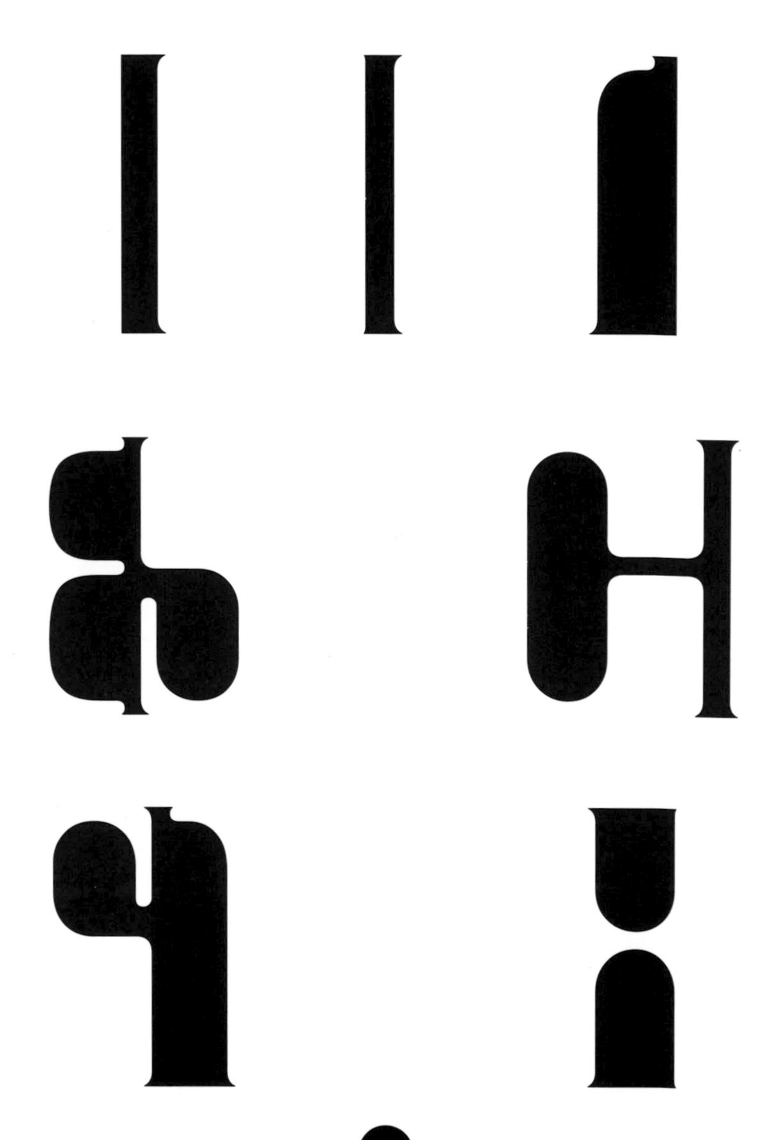

Following the logic of the arrows at all times, how many routes are there from Start to Finish?

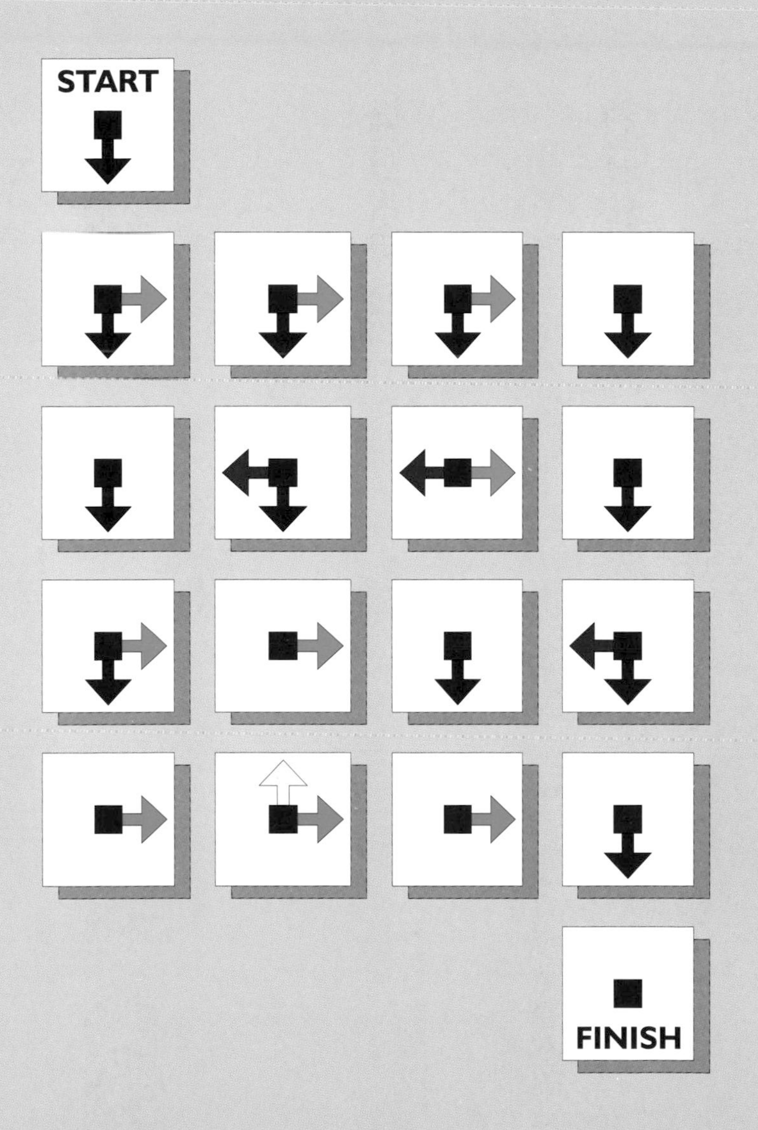

In order to continue the logic, should Z be red or blue?

A	B	C	D	E
F	G	H	I	J
K	L	M	N	O
P	Q	R	S	T
U	V	W	X	Y

?

Here are six cryptic symbols in a sequence which has been formed using simple geometric operations.

Which of these six symbols would also appear as the seventh symbol?

If all the blocks except the correct three are shaded out, something that does not exist will appear before your eyes.

Connect like with like using four continuous lines which must not cross or go through any of the diamonds.

Follow-up: Is it always possible to perform this even if the middle diamonds are arranged in a different way?

Pair up these pictures. There is a common logic that runs throughout all the pairs.

Rotate the wheels to form a word.

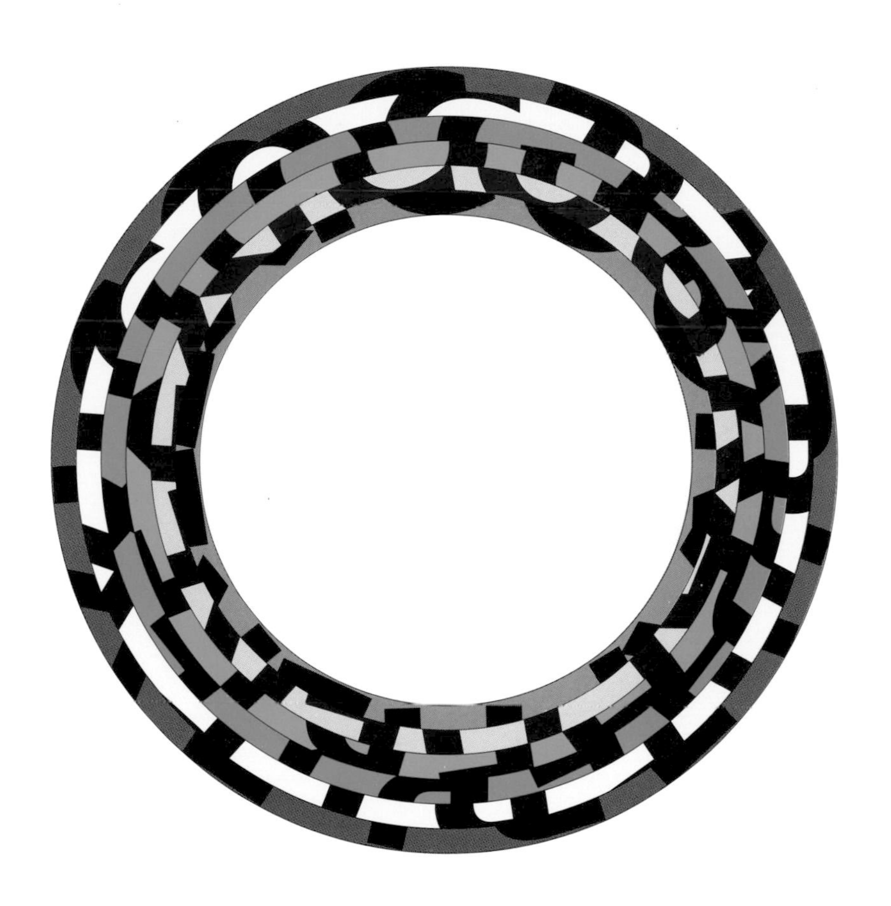

Shade these hexagons in red, yellow, blue and green so that:

1) There are at least three hexagons of each type.

2) Each green shares a border with exactly three red hexagons.

3) Each blue shares a border with exactly two yellow hexagons.

4) Each yellow shares a border with at least one red, one green and one blue hexagon.

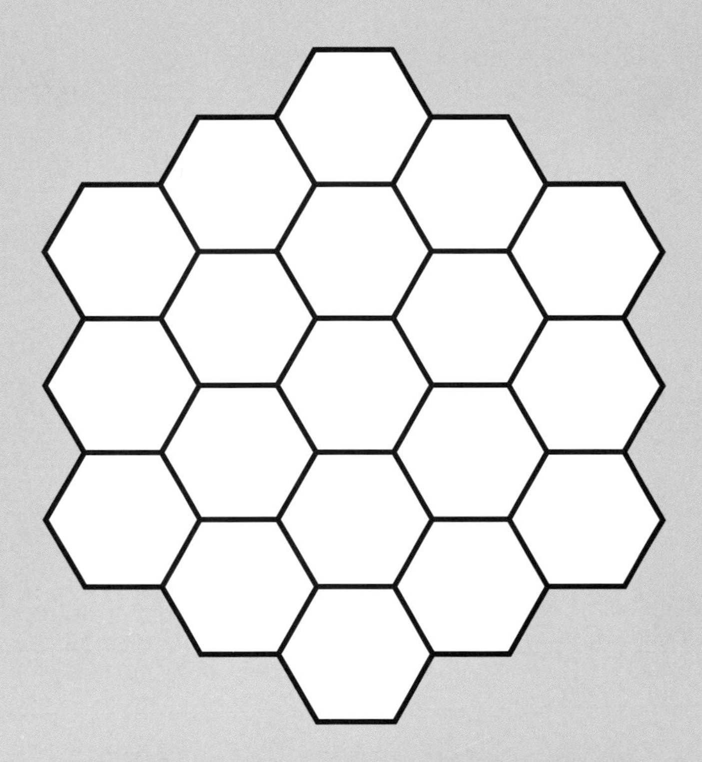

This is the world's easiest maze, in that there is only one route to the finish. However, you must obey a particular rule.

You must move either four or seven squares, forwards or backwards, each time, so that you have landed on every letter before you reach the finish.

What is the successful route?

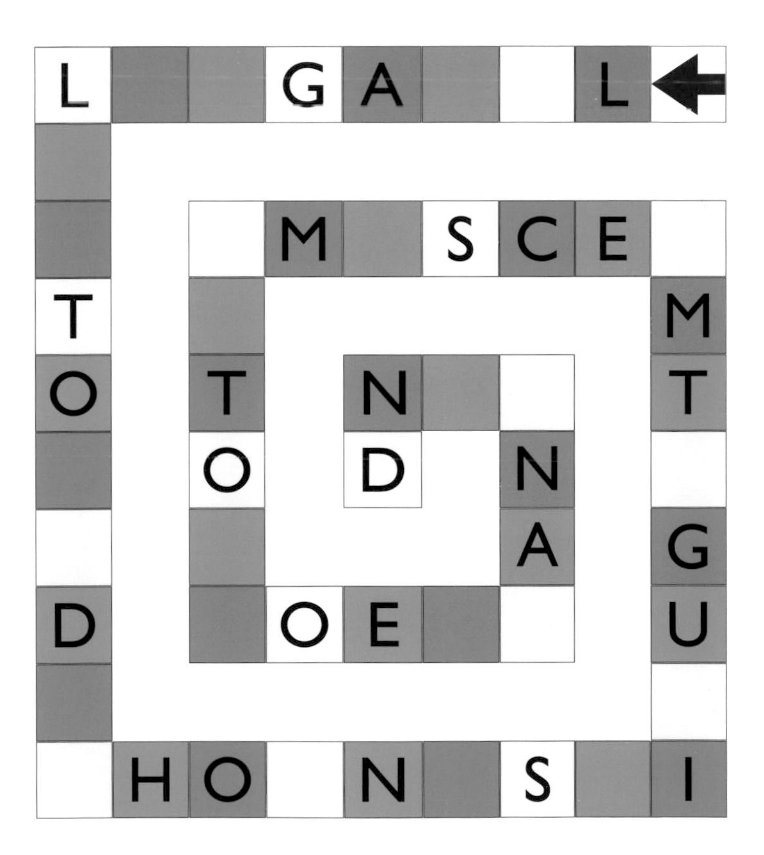

This is a very difficult puzzle, but with a little linear thought it is not impossible.

What number should appear in the final circle?

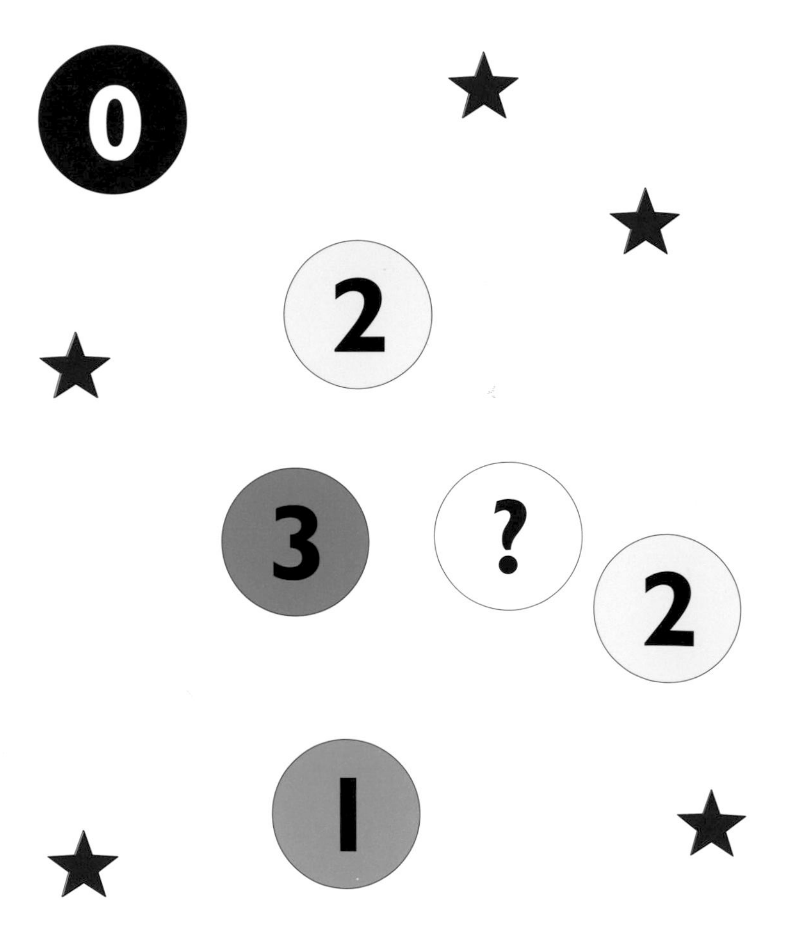

While your mind's eye is trying to work out whether the circle on the left or the right is the top one, here's a number teaser to think about:

Suppose these circles were drawn with lines of negligible thickness. How many separate areas have been formed by this figure?

Rotate the rings so that six words, all beginning with O, can be read outwards along the windmill's sails.

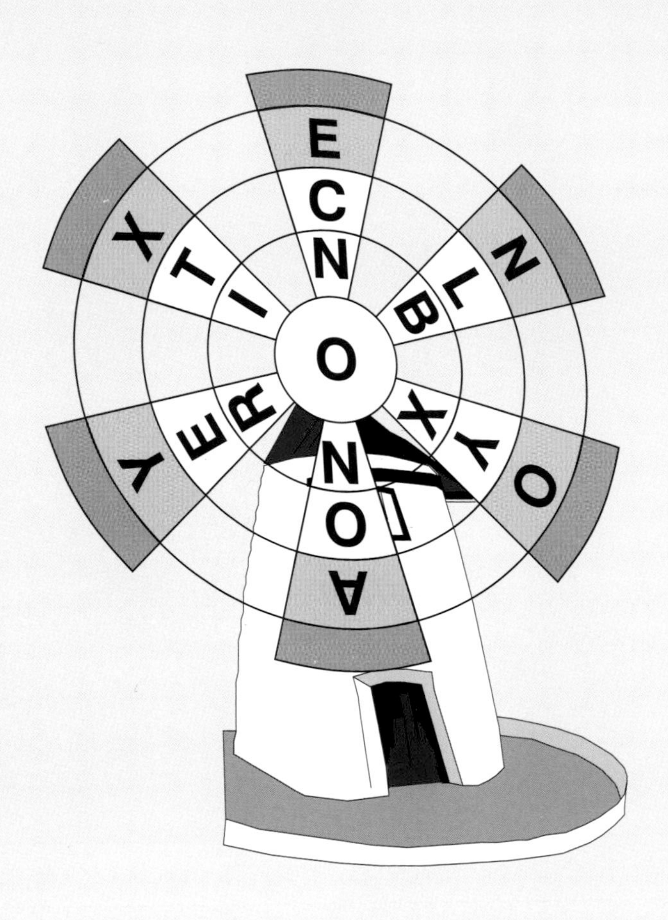

Which type of ball should appear in the position indicated by the question mark?

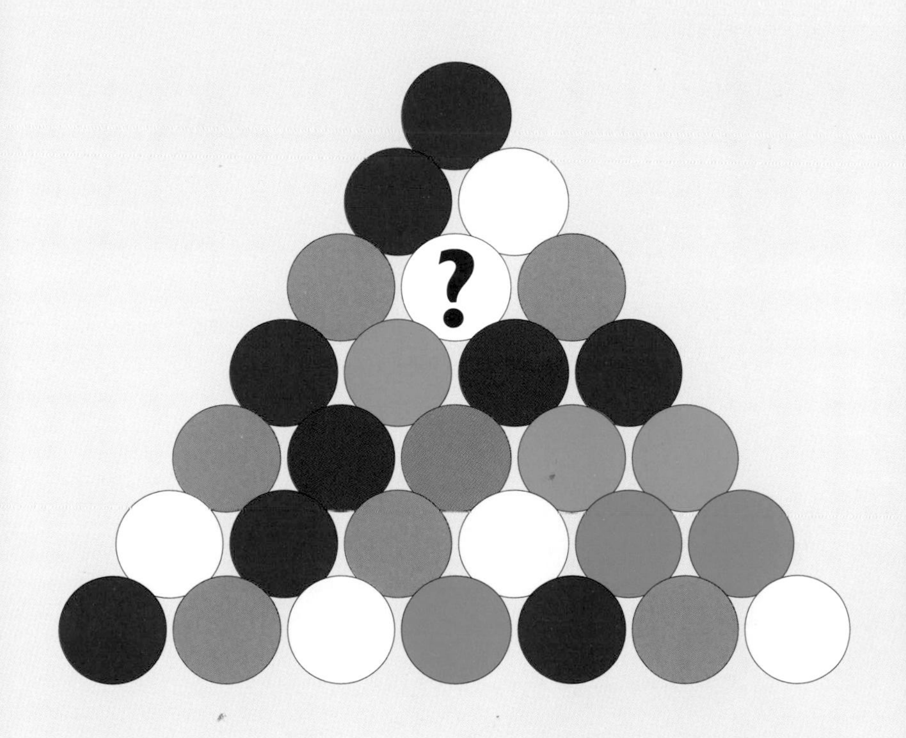

In this rather bizarre puzzle, your first aim is to identify the famous people.

Then work out which three had a profession in common.

Place these letter roundels on the grid so that, no matter which route you choose from the top row to bottom, you can always form a four-letter word.

As a starter clue, the second row are all vowels and no two circles connected by a line share anything in common.

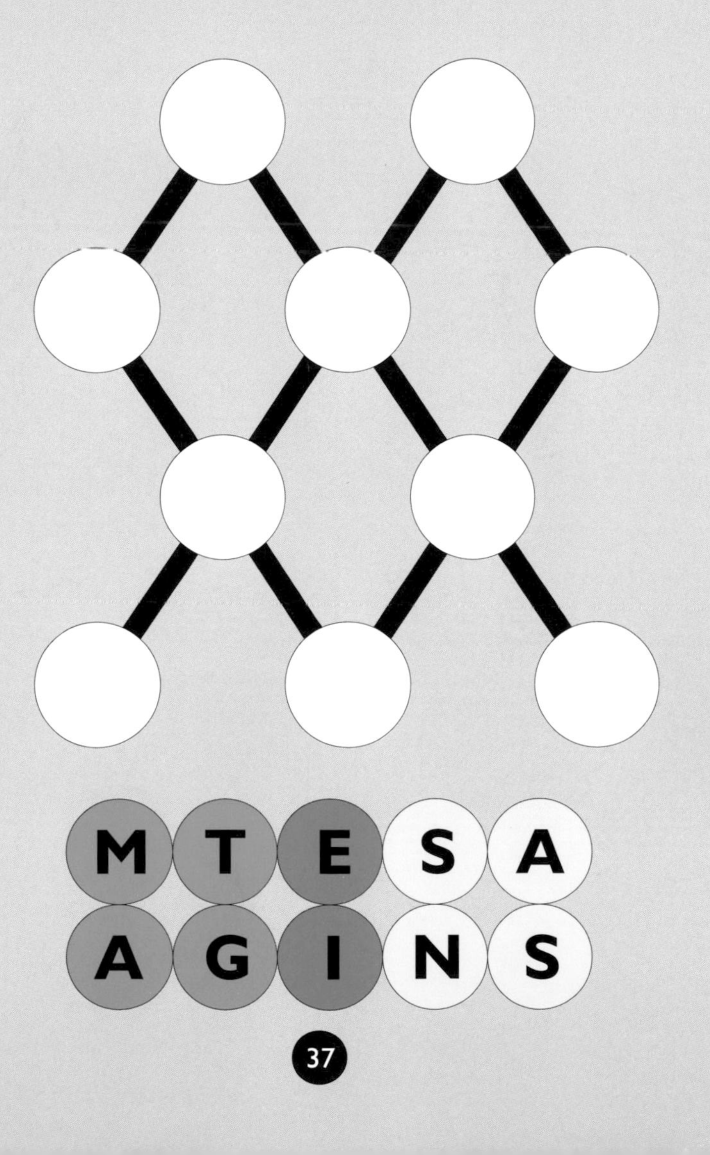

This is an illusion known as *Schroeder's staircase*. To appreciate why it's special, try turning the book upside down.

Rearrange the cards, one yellow and one blue per step, so that the totals on all five steps are five consecutive numbers (e.g. 6, 7, 8, 9, 10).

Crack the safe by deciding whether the statements below are true or false. This will lead to the correct two-digit code number.

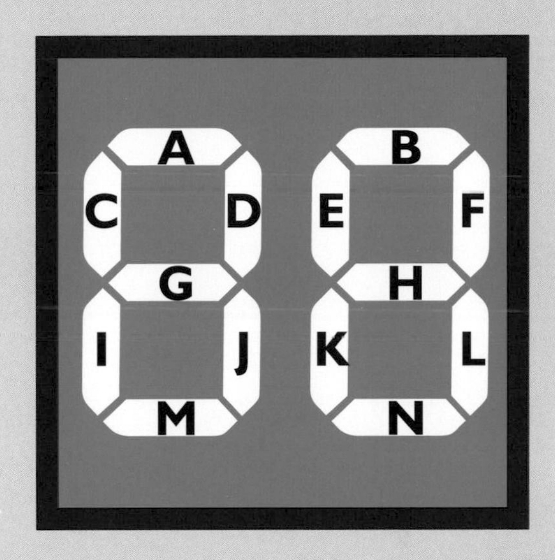

A) Shirley Bassey sung the theme for the film "Live and Let Die"
B) A methuselah holds the equivalent of 8 bottles of champagne
C) Boxer Marvin Hagler's nickname is "Marvellous Marvin"
D) The last day of the year is December 31st
E) Nova Scotia is a state of Canada
F) The capital of Morocco is Harare
G) The chemical symbol for Barium is Ba
H) A Pina Colada contains coconut milk
I) Casemate is a losing position in chess
J) The collective noun for kittens is a "kindle"
K) The Garfield cartoon is drawn by Miles Davis
L) Cambodia used to be called Kampuchea
M) Flyweight is the lightest boxing weight
N) The currency of Denmark is the krone

How's your geography? Starting with the large C each time, can you spell out the names of six French towns and cities by driving along the roads.

Letters can be re-used for different towns.

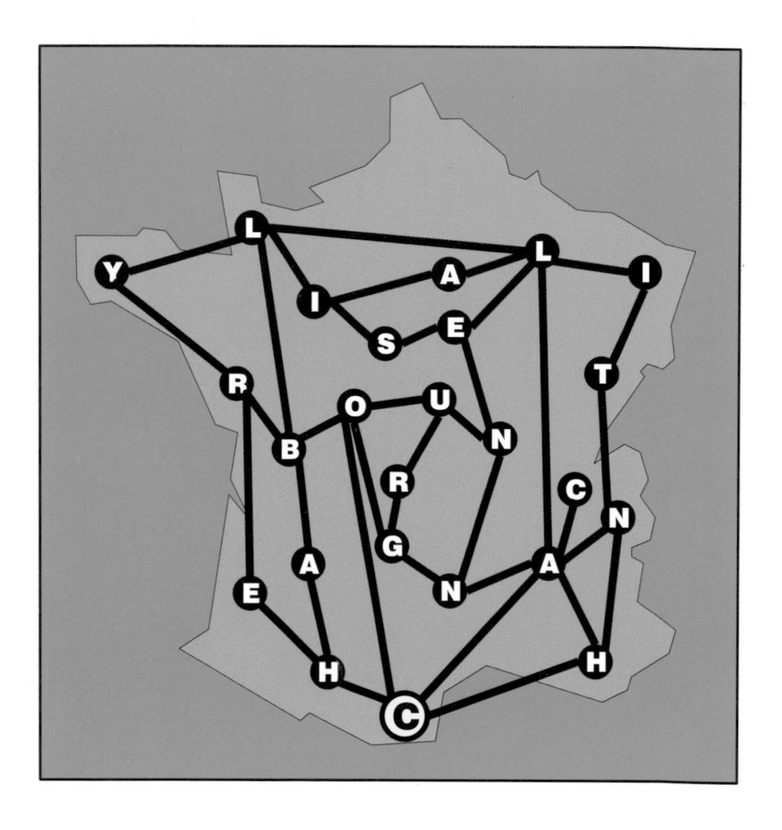

Starting at the green octagon, make your way to the finish. However, throughout your journey you must apply the same logic at each step.

Pair up one picture on the left with one picture on the right. Which pair is different from the others?

Of these six diagrams, which ones can you trace without going over any line twice or taking your pen off the paper at any stage?

… Following on from the previous question, see if you can trace the Olympic flag symbol using the same set of rules.

The bricks in this wall are absolutely rectangular, even though the lines appear slanted.

How many ways are there of getting from brick A to brick B using 8 yellow and 9 blue bricks, inclusive of A and B?

What word should go into the final box?

TRAFFIC

LITMUS

SUNBURN

?

I live at A, and a friend of mine lives at B. What are the *simplest possible* directions I can tell my friend, so that she can drive to my house using the road layout shown?

The route she takes need not be the shortest possible in terms of distance.

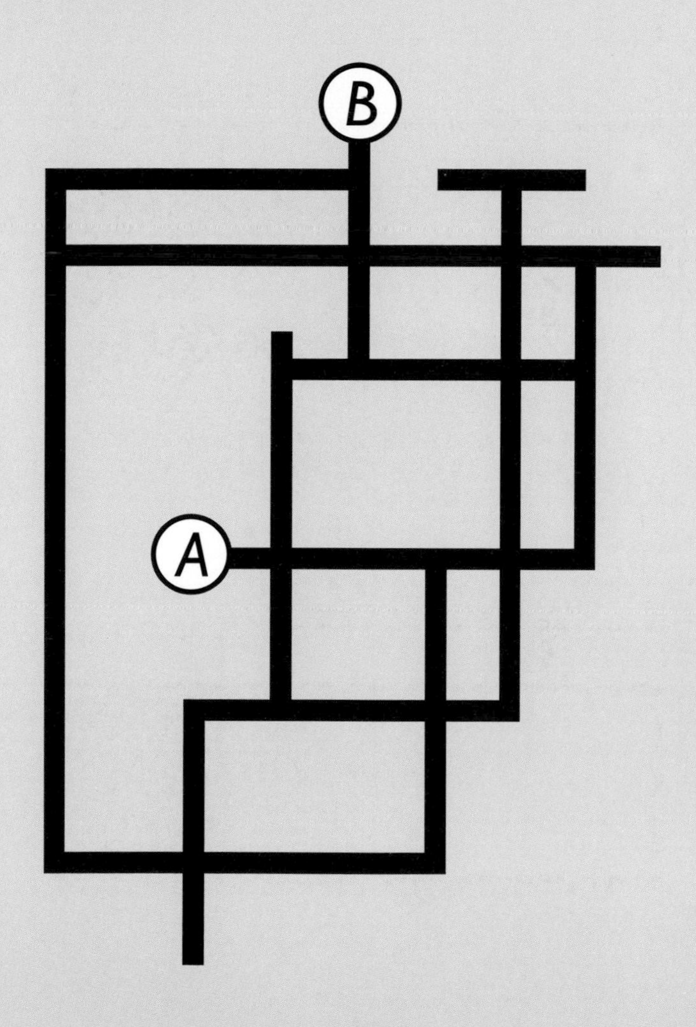

This is one of the sliding block puzzles I used to play with when I was younger.

How many moves away am I from completing it? A move consists of moving a row or column of tiles (or part of one).

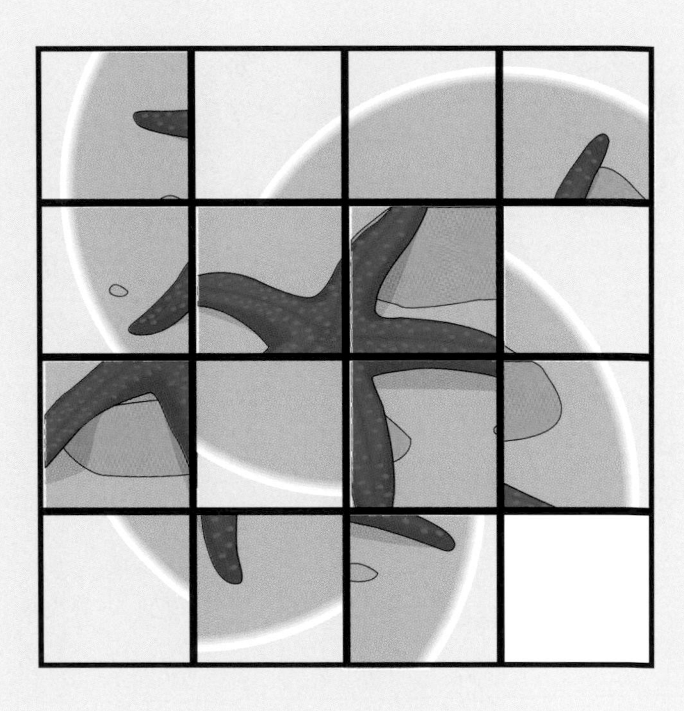

Turn four of these circles through 180 degrees each to create an illusion of a well-known geometric figure.

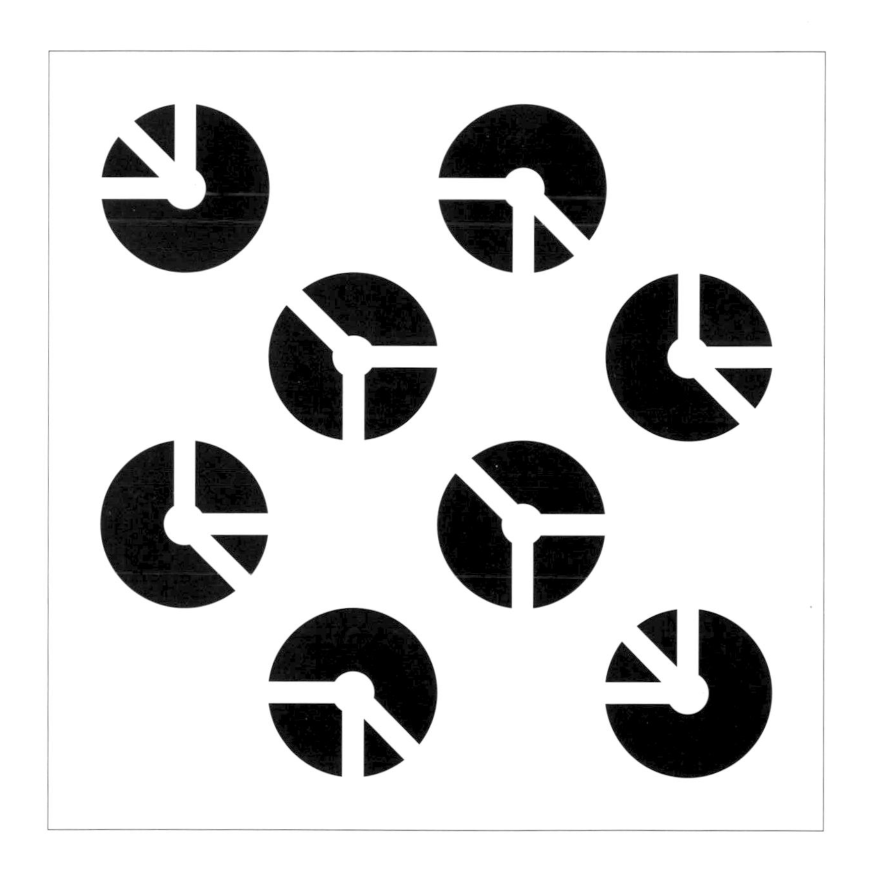

Connect like to like using continuous lines. You are only allowed to draw one line through each narrow gap behind the circles.

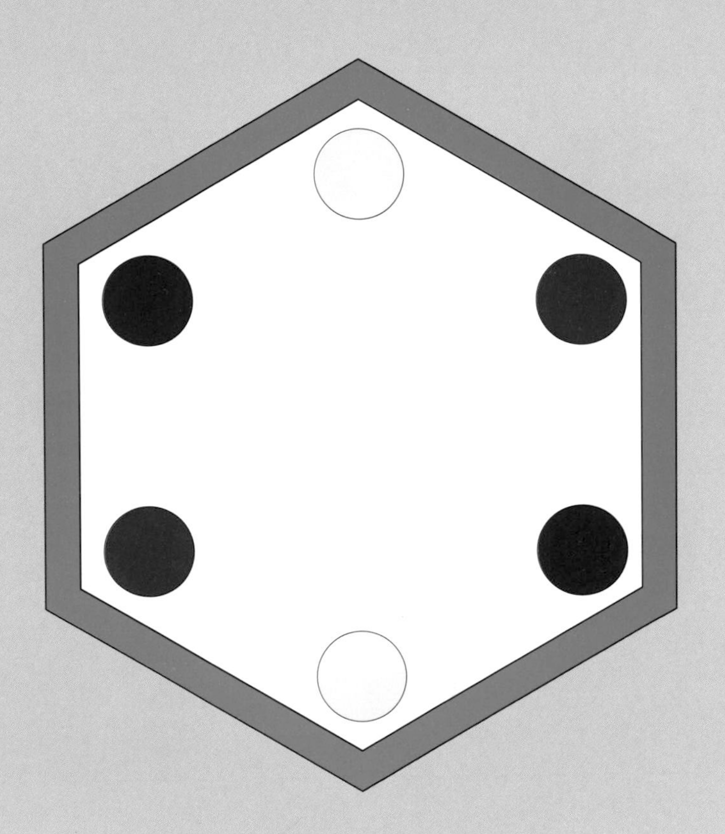

The Sultan is very pleased with his new rug, which is in the shape of three connected hexagons:

However, he wants to be equally pleased with his new tiled floor that is about to be installed. The workmen are poised with ten yellow, blue and green tiles, which will be placed in the grid shown. He is delighted that there is an equal number of each type of tile.

How can the workmen install the tiled floor so that, *regardless* of where the Sultan places his rug, there is always an equal number (i.e. nine) of each tile left visible?

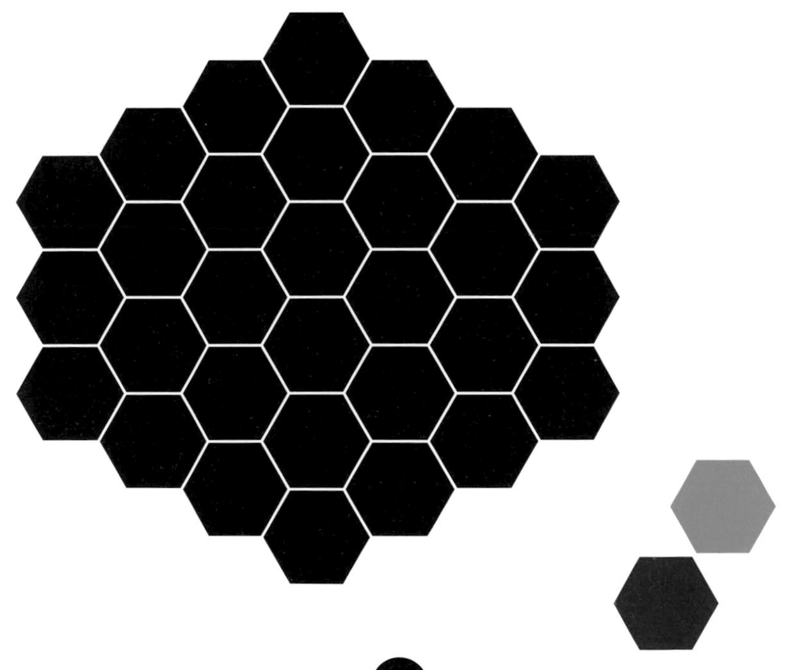

This is a two stage puzzle. First, continue the logic that we have started off for you here.

Then work out what the dots signify. This will give you the final, four-letter answer.

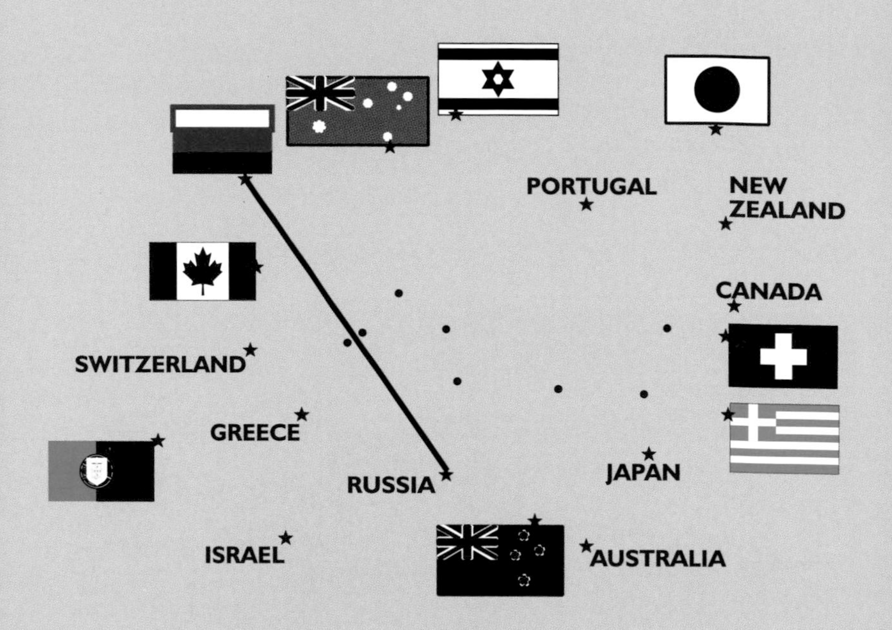

What's the link between these four pictures?

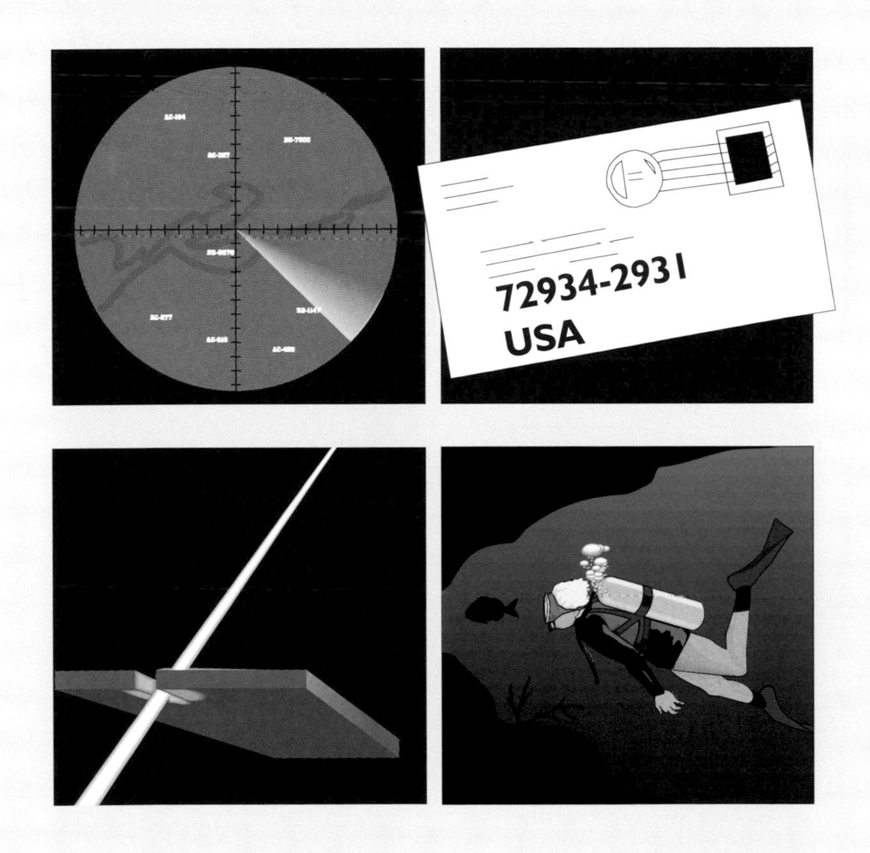

Can you work out the logic that is being used here, and thus supply either of the two letters that can satisfy the final equation?

$$D + M = R$$

$$X - N = C$$

$$(K + R) \div R = T$$

$$(B \times W) + E = Y$$

$$R \times N \times A = H + X$$

$$(X \div G) + F - K = ?$$

Turn this book side-to-side while looking at this figure, and strange radial lines will appear.

And if that isn't puzzling enough, solve the maze.

You have a weighing balance with two pans. The position of 13 identical gold coins is shown.

Given that each pan weighs the same as one gold coin, move only **one** coin so that the scales balance exactly.

This is a diagram of the one-way system near to where I live. My house is at A, and I am trying to get to work at B. I have a choice of routes at the ends of some stretches of road, but when I make my choice I must follow the road around, and keep progressing in the same direction.

What route should I choose?

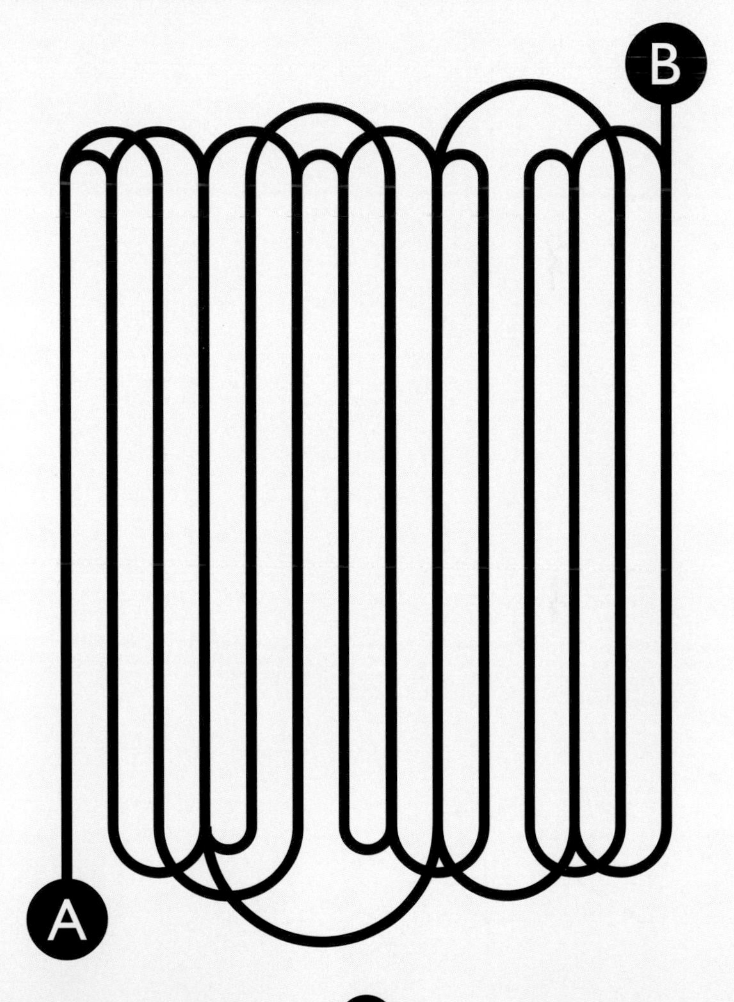

Place the remaining letters on the circles so that two words can be read around each circle: one clockwise, the other counterclockwise.

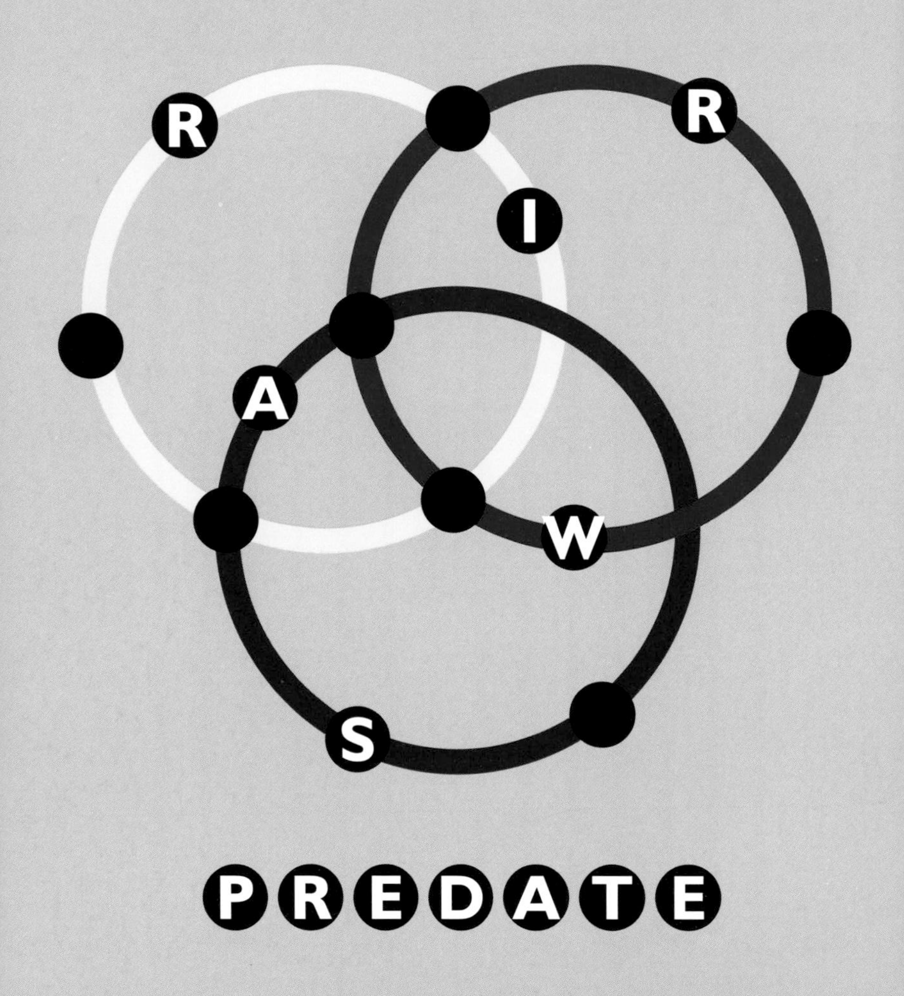

Use continuous black lines to join like to like, without ever going outside the main octagon, or crossing another line or octagon.

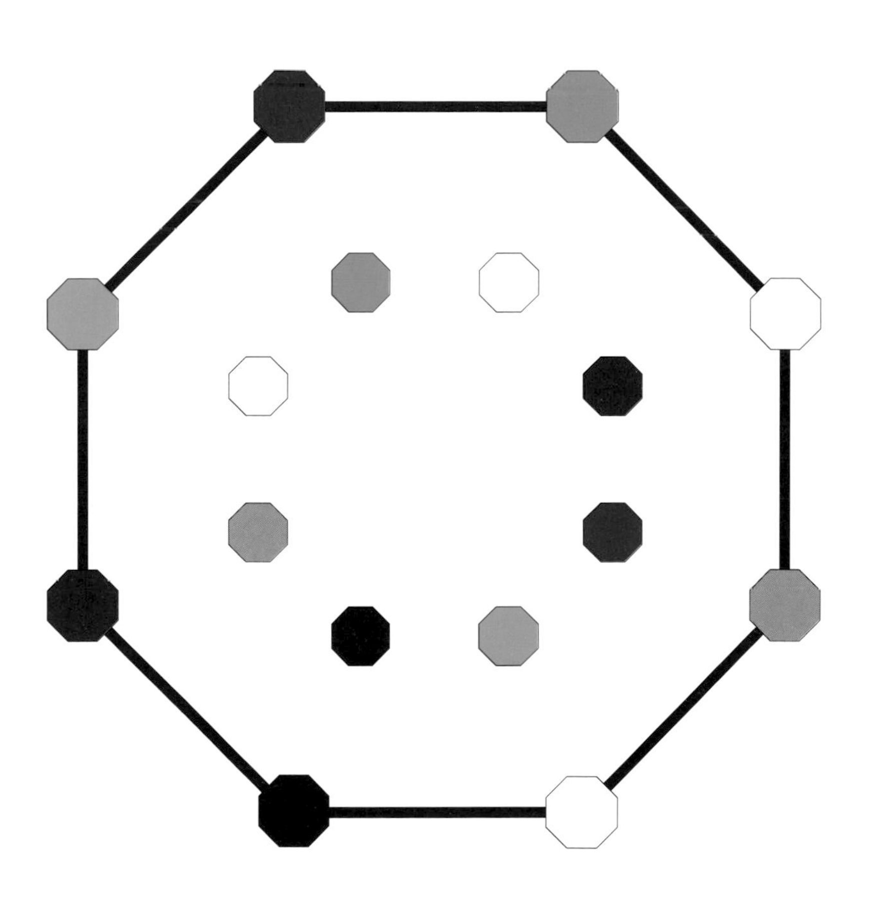

This puzzle uses a well-known optical illusion. In each case, select the arrow head that you think goes with each flight.

What four-letter word can be made from the letters you have selected?

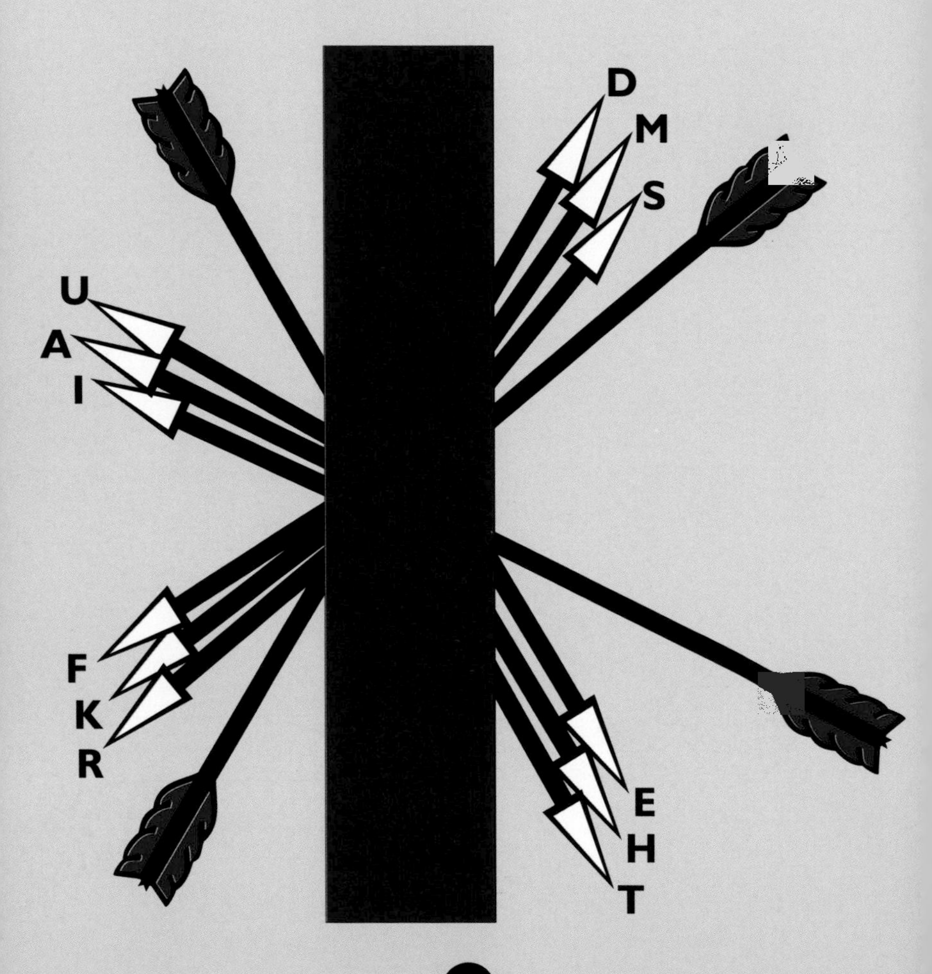

I asked someone to put together a few pictures for a new puzzle I'd invented. However, they came back with these instead, which are completely different and are unsuitable for the picture crossword I was planning.

Why are all these pictures not what I expected?

Here is a crossword clue:

Geometric shape (3 letters)

Which of the options below satisfies this clue?

This is a cross-section of a Yale lock. The height of the pins depends on each part of the key inserted into the lock.

Why wouldn't this arrangement of pins make a good lock?

A cue ball is struck from the white pocket of this pool table at an angle of 45 degrees. The pool table is X feet long, and Y feet across, where X and Y are whole numbers. Assume that the cue ball never runs out of energy, and that the cushions do not alter the natural angle of rebound.

In which pocket will the ball fall into if:

(a) X is 6, and Y is 5

(b) X is 13, and Y is 10

(c) X is 4137, and Y is 2091

Using only your mind's eye to help you, can you envisage how these arrows can be fitted together, nose-to-tail, in order to form a continuous loop?

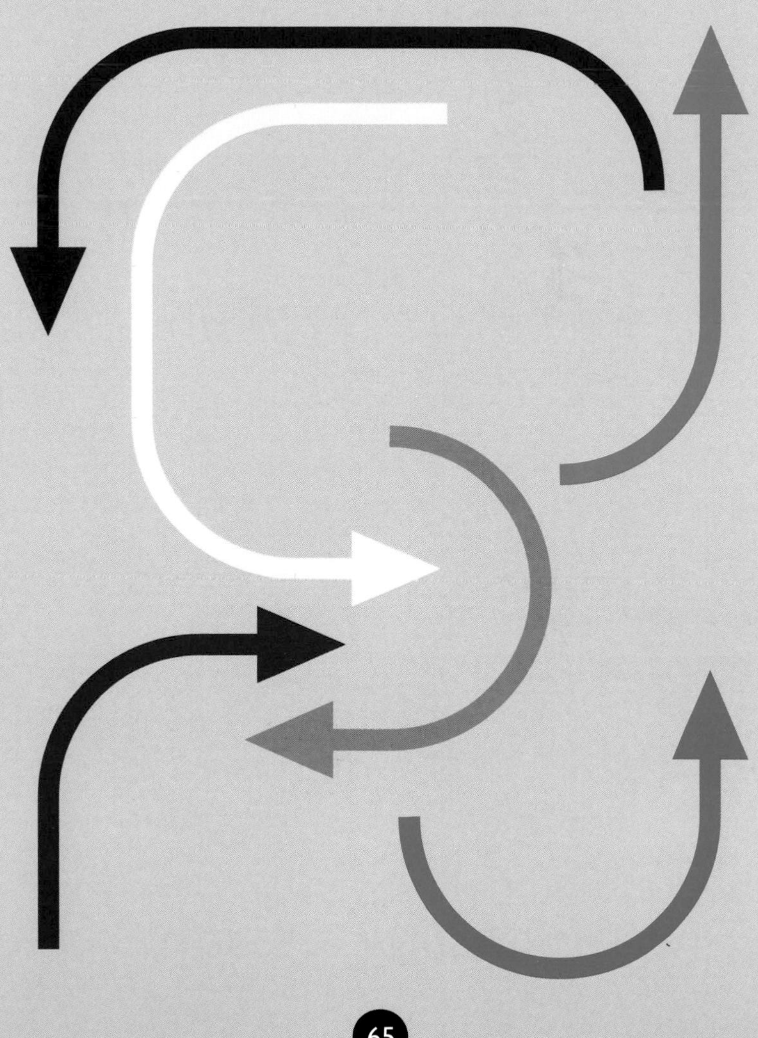

What word is being hidden here?

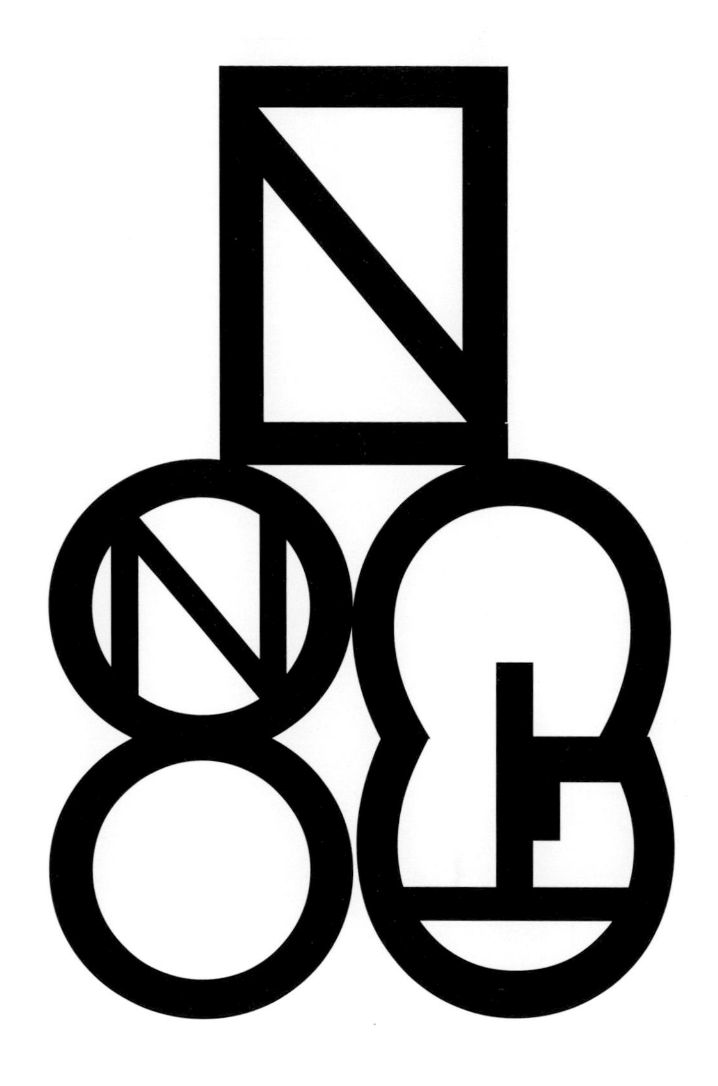

Choose only three of the clear glass pieces and place them into the grid so that each row forms the same total.

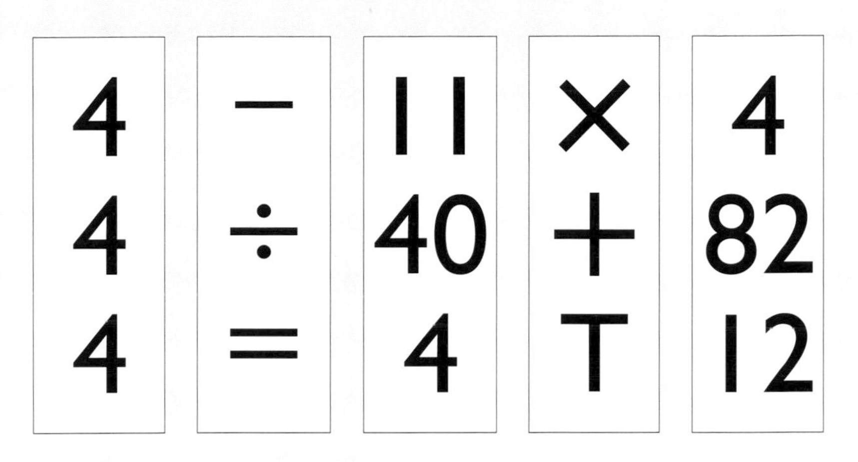

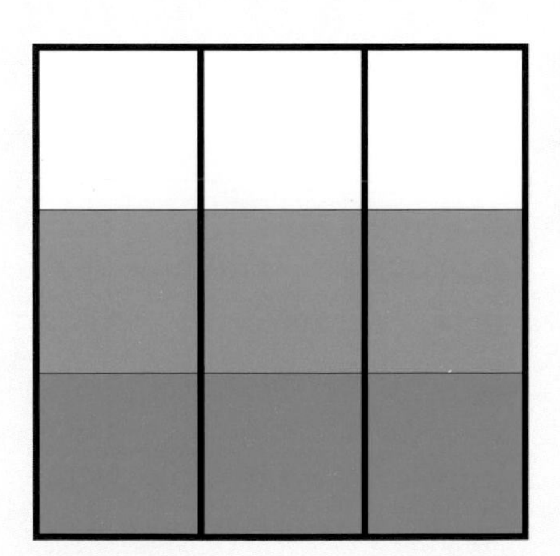

What's true, and what's false?

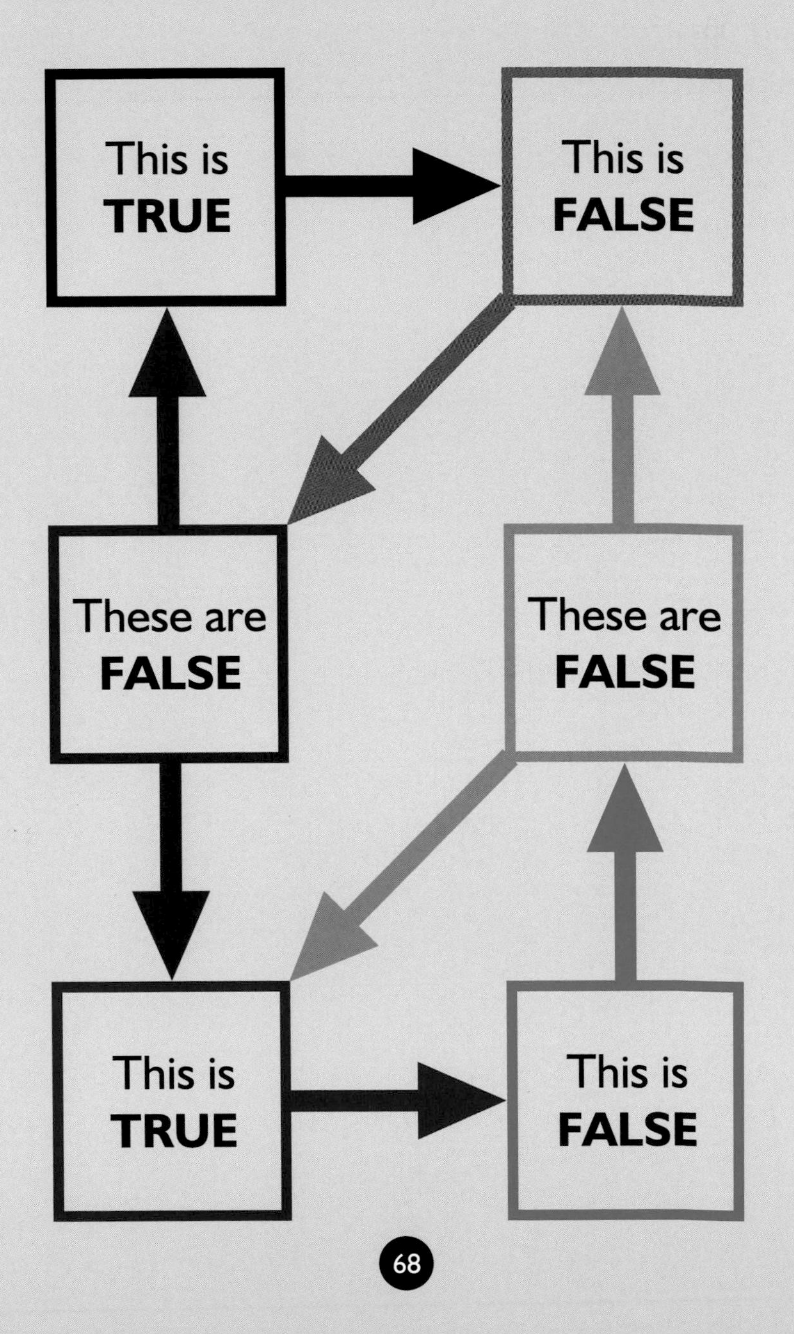

What is the smallest number of columns that you need to turn upside-down in so that each row contains the exactly same set of symbols as the other rows?

What is the minimum number of letters you need to swap on this coat hanger in order to obtain a word of at least six letters in length?

How should the yellow, green and blue tiles be rearranged so that the ordering of the letters is reversed, as illustrated?

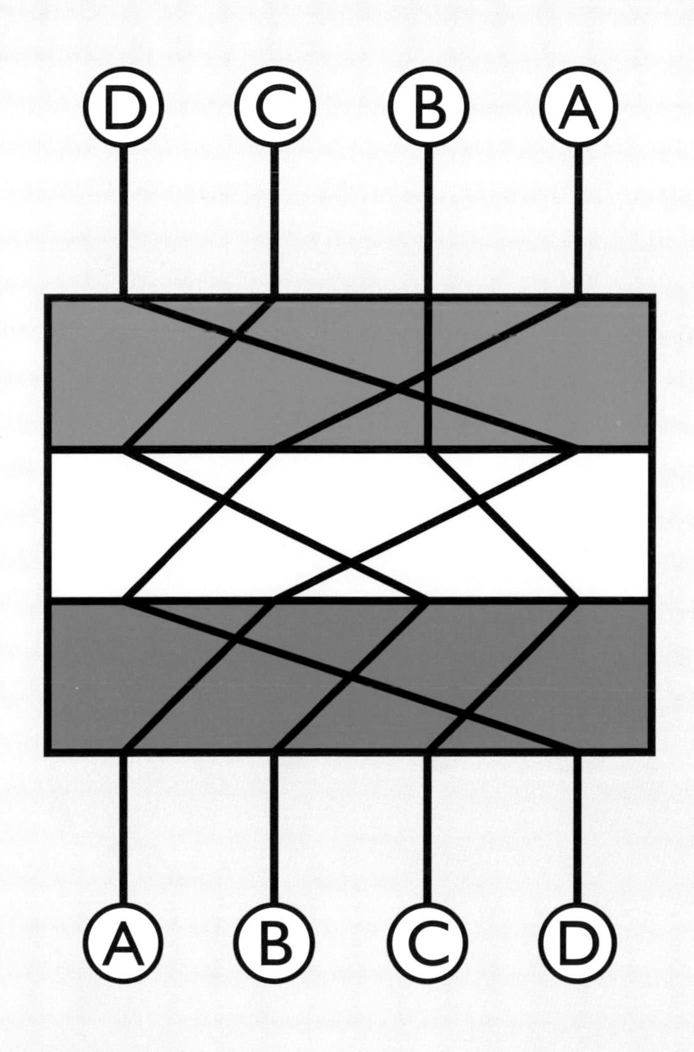

A "play" symbol on this remote control means move one square in that direction, and a "fast forward/rewind" symbol means move two squares.

How many ways are there of getting from OFF to ON? To solve this systematically, start with the buttons near OFF and determine how many routes there are to them. Then work your way towards ON.

Place eight more dots on the grid lines so that both these conditions hold:

(a) Every horizontal and vertical line contains three dots.

(b) The boundary of each of the nine small squares contains three dots.

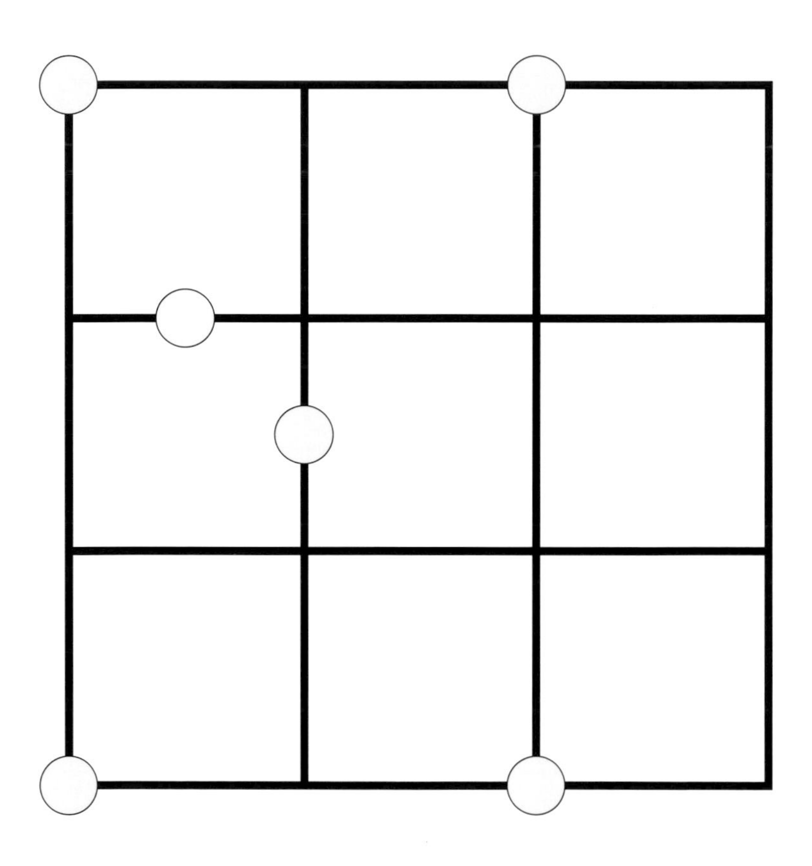

There is a valuable gold ball in this rotatable maze, which is mounted on a wall. There is a catch – I will charge you £1 for every 90 degrees counterclockwise you turn the maze. The good news is clockwise revolutions are free. The ball has a large inertia, and only starts to move once your turn has been made.

What is the minimum amount you'd need to pay to release the ball?

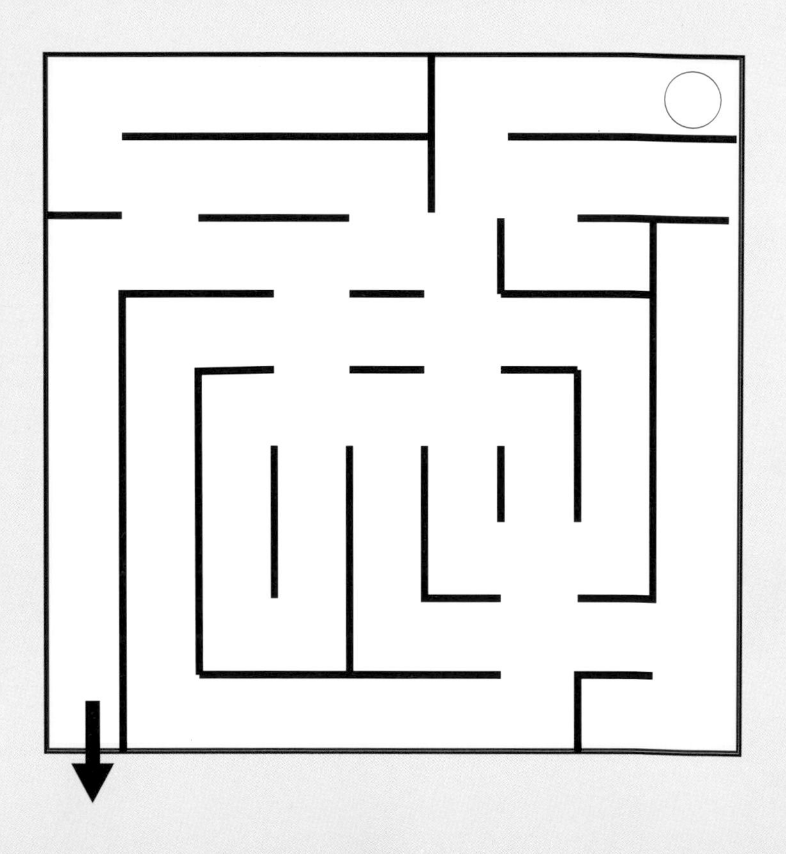

Each letter has been lined up against the correct row or column in which it appears.

Position the letters so that *every* row and column contains letters which, when rearranged, give something connected with food and drink.

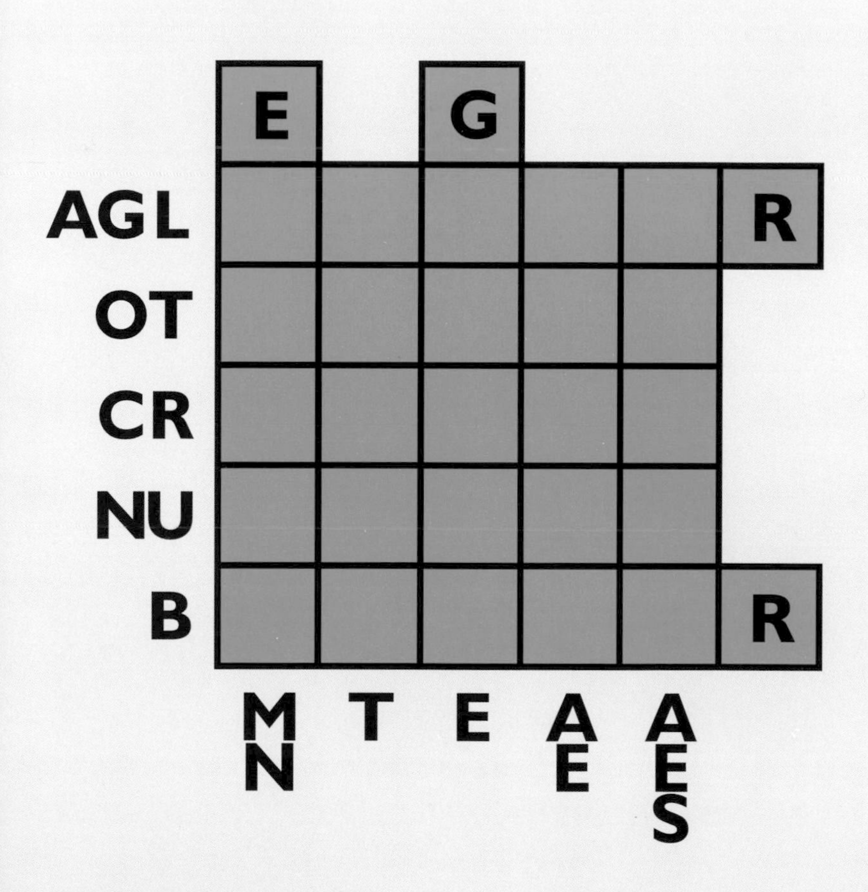

The man who runs the local video shop near my house fancies himself as a bit of cryptologist. Instead of the usual jackets on the video boxes, he puts rebuses on them for people to work out.

Can you see what films I'm hiring here?

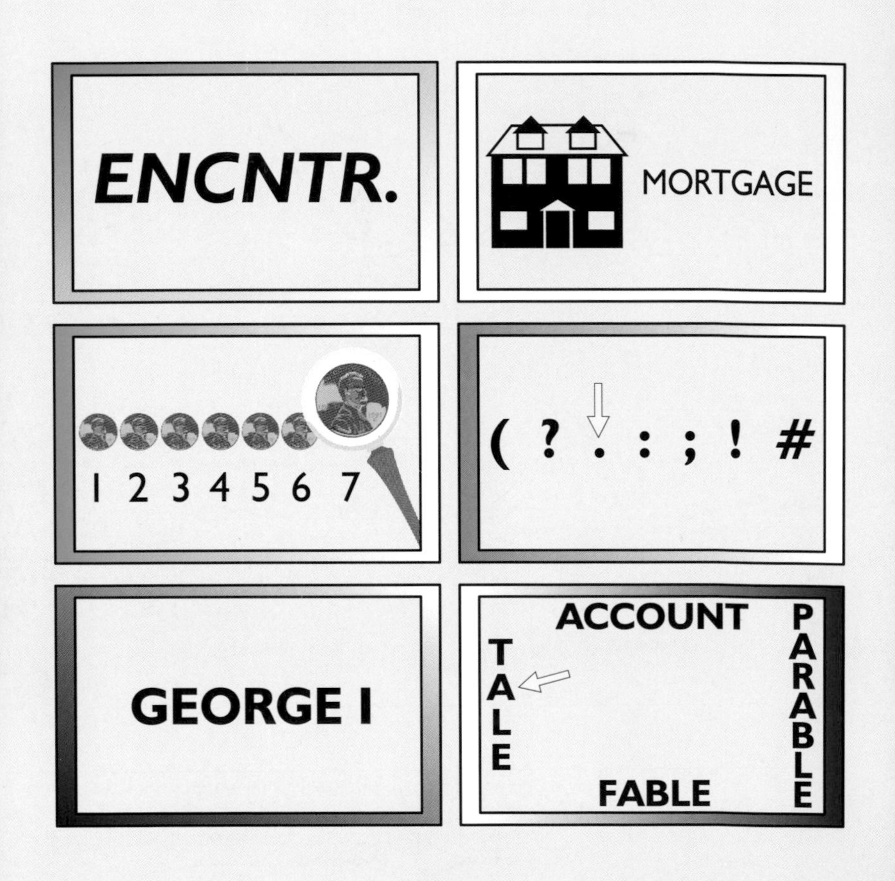

Start at the yellow triangle, and keep adding numbers all the way. You may use the red arrows once, and the blue arrows twice, but the same arrow cannot be used consecutively.

Which route through the arrows gives you the desired total?

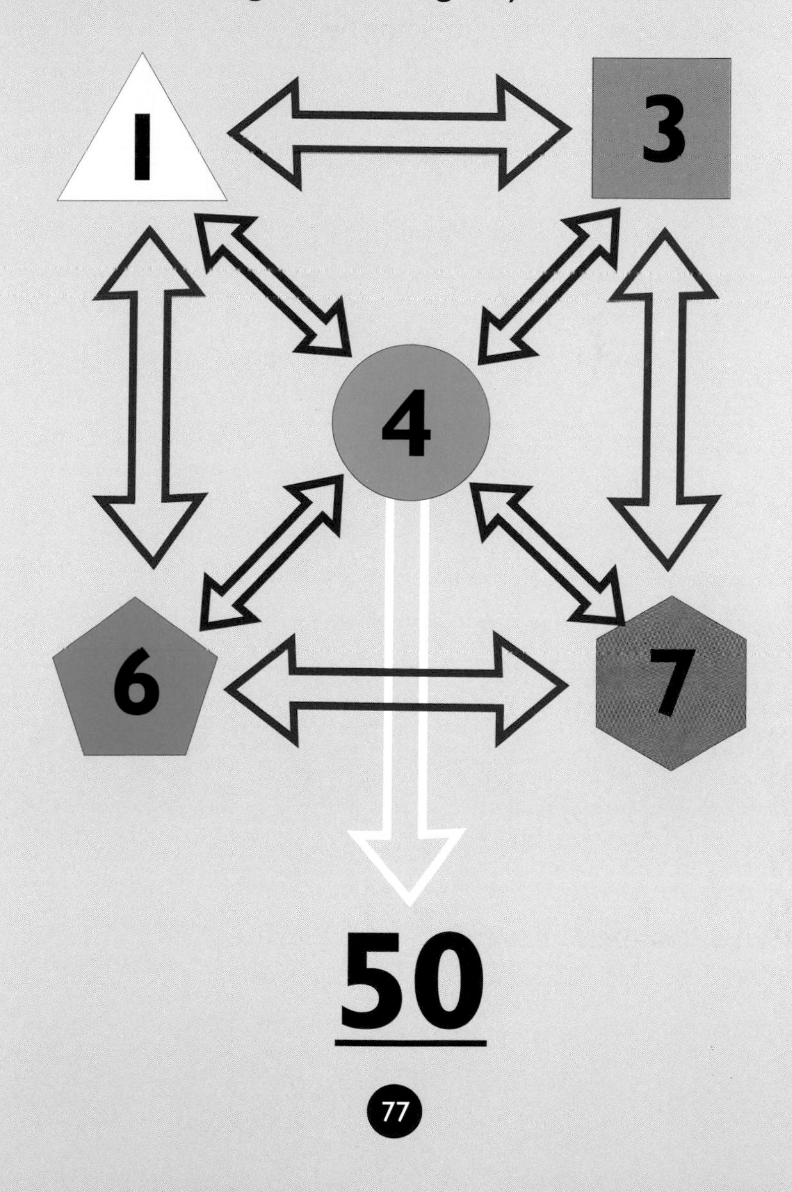

Which point in this network takes longest to get to, if you start from the top corner and always travel in the direction of the arrows?

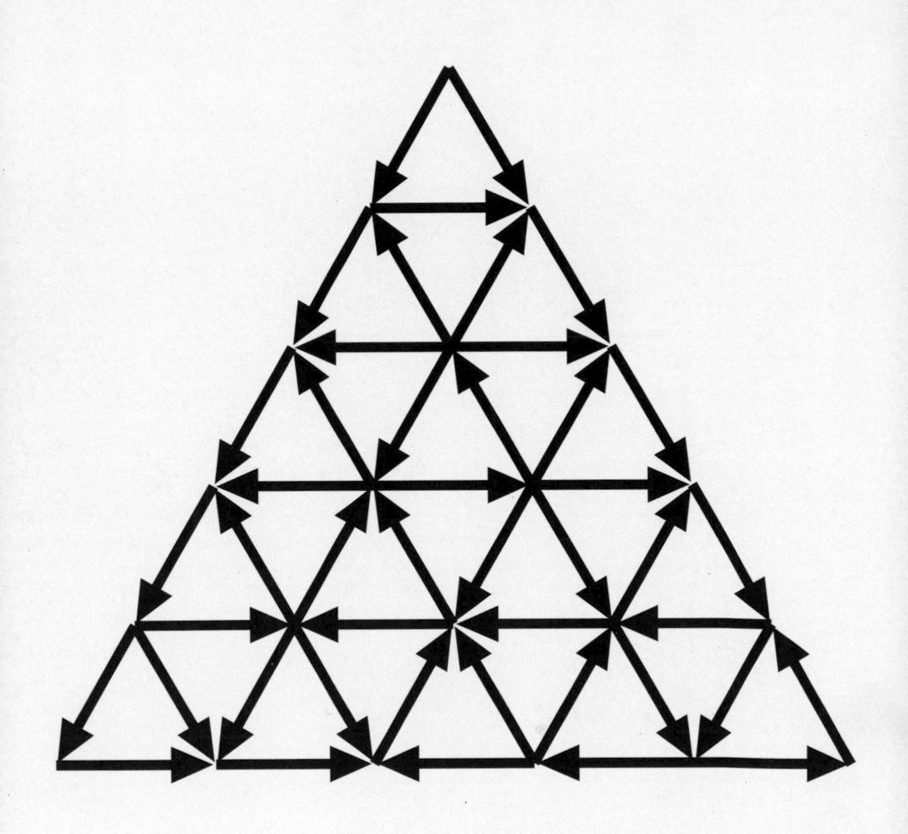

What is the link between these pictures?

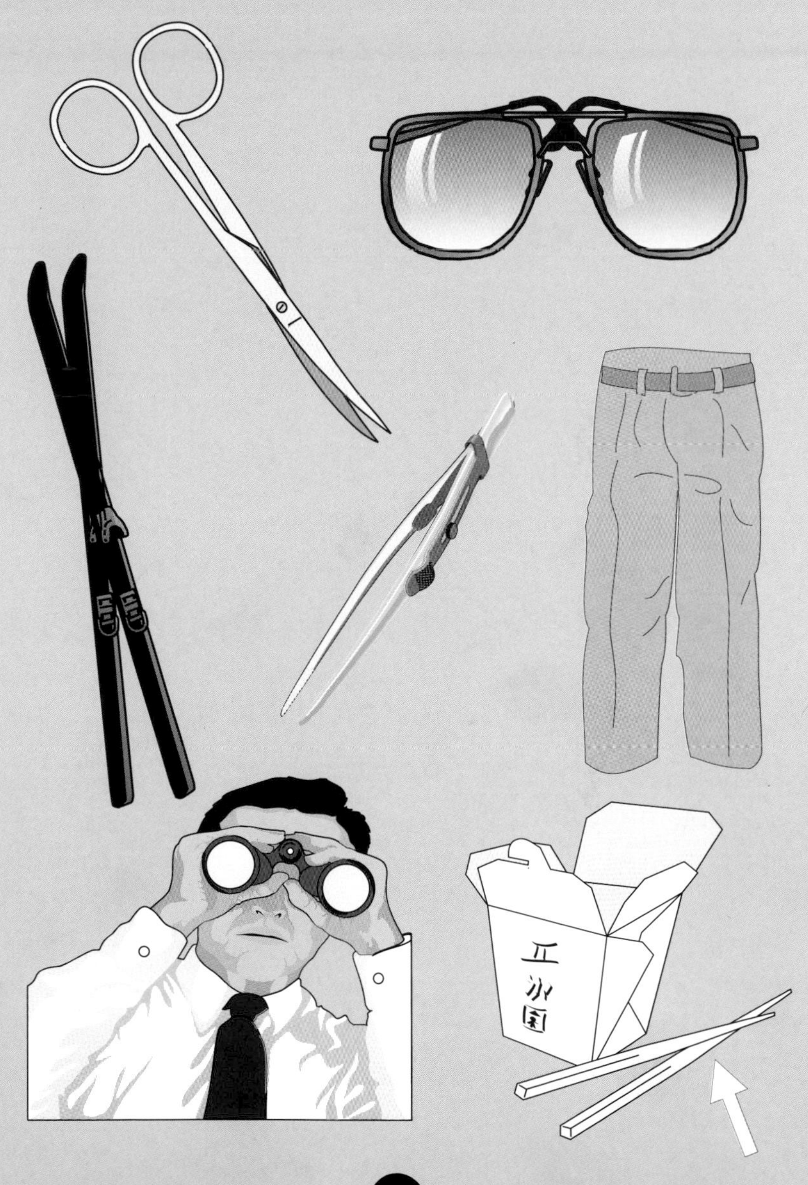

A happy face, a grumpy face, a couple of scythes, and some strange squiggles.

What have these optical illusions got in common?

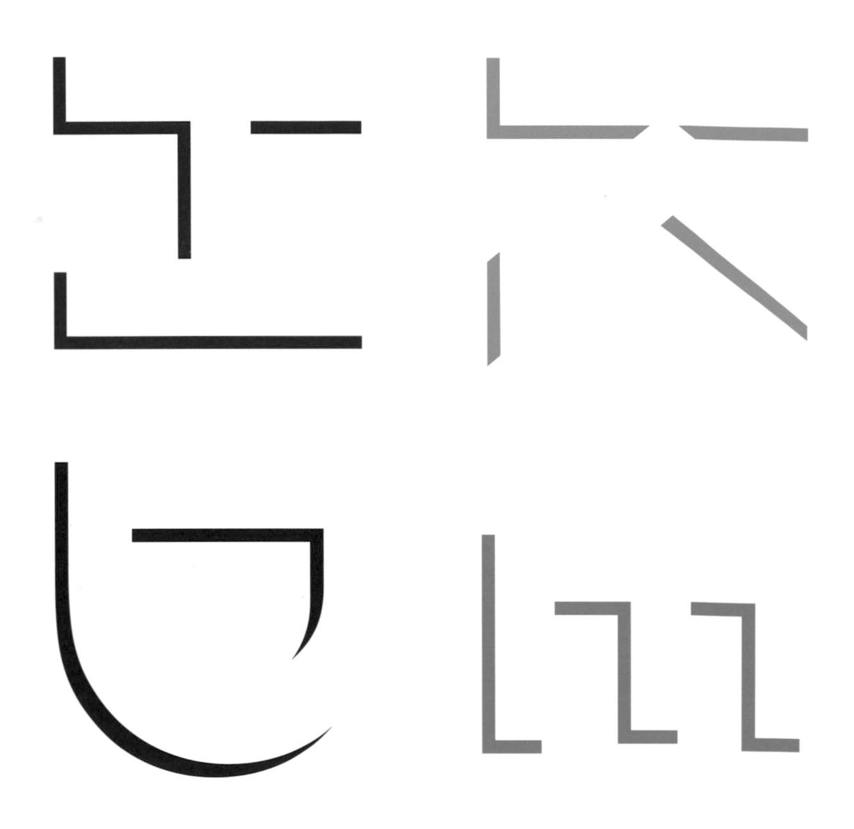

Which of the symbols is the odd one out, and can you also say precisely why it is the misfit?

If the "T" cogwheel is revolved at three revolutions per minute, how long will it take before the word "SYNTAX" is once again correctly displayed on these cogwheels?

S has 12 teeth
Y has 15 teeth
N has 16 teeth
T has 20 teeth
A has 22 teeth
X has 28 teeth

If you stare at this optical illusion, you will find that your eyes want to form geometric patterns of smaller groups of dots, because the eye cannot take in the whole picture at once.

Suppose you want to get from the green side to the blue side using a route formed of exactly 11 consecutive circles (i.e. no "jumping" allowed). How many different routes are available to you?

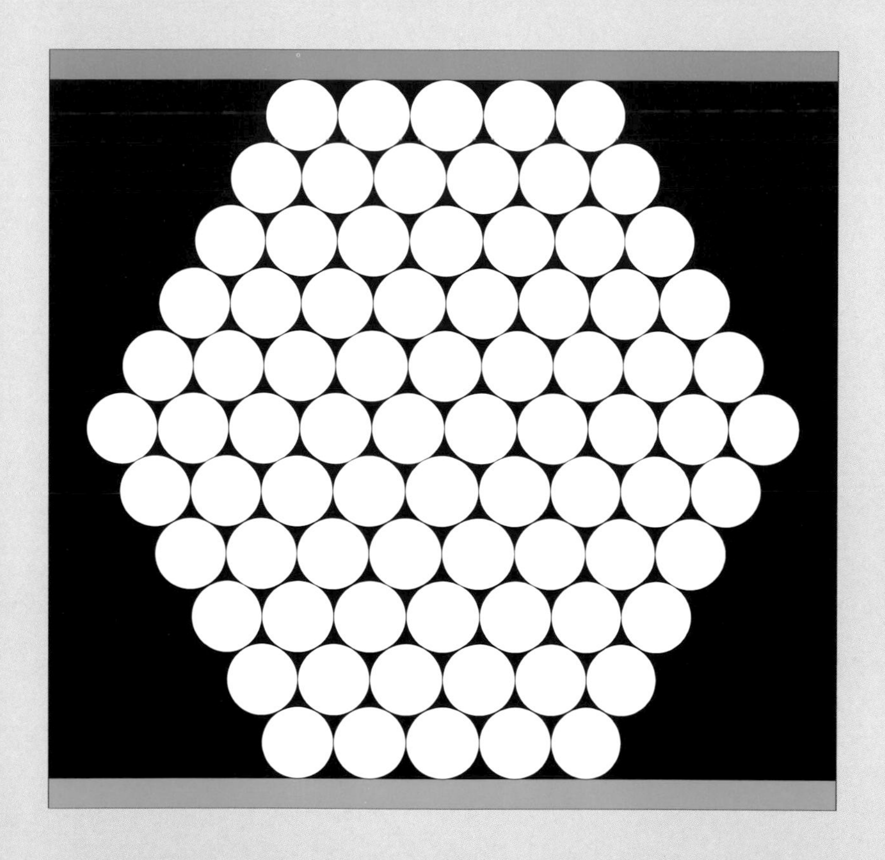

Can you get from A to B? You may not travel between any pair of matching arrows.

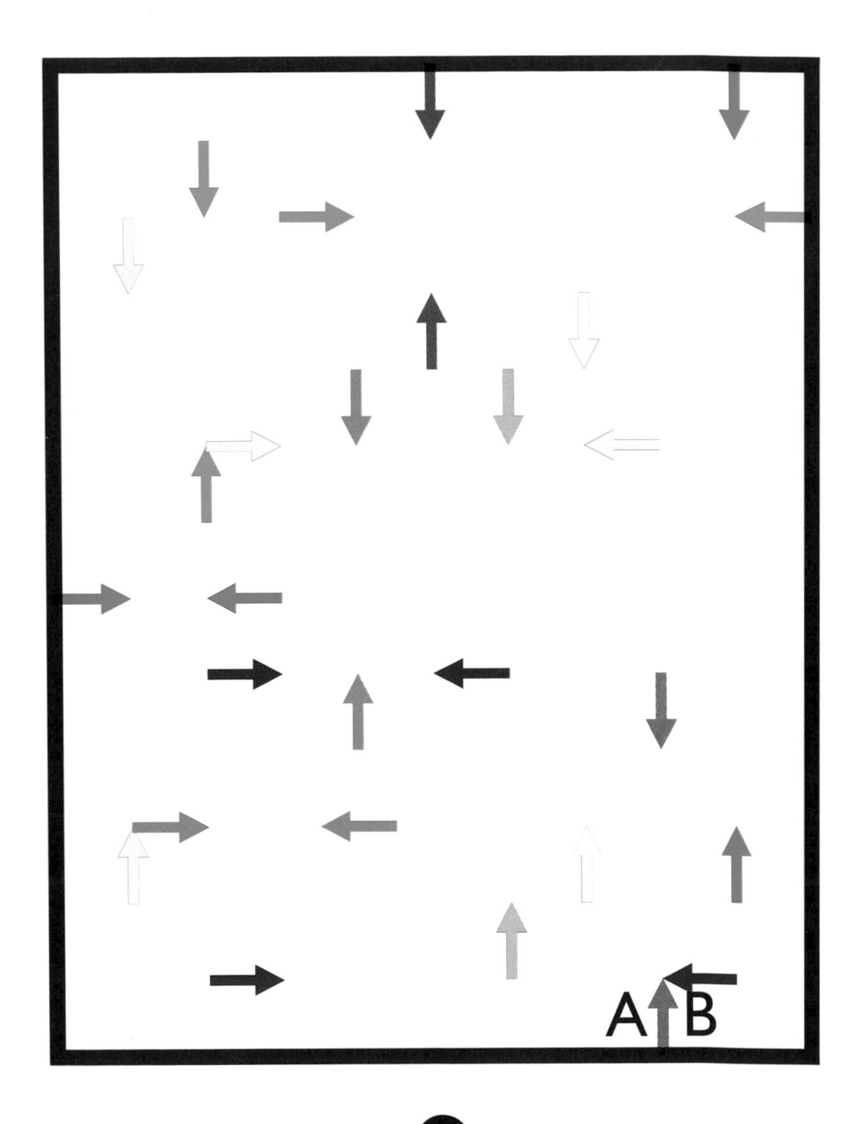

Place the weights on the pans so that the entire system is in balance (in other words, all three poles are completely horizontal).

Assume that the pans and the rods are of negligible weight.

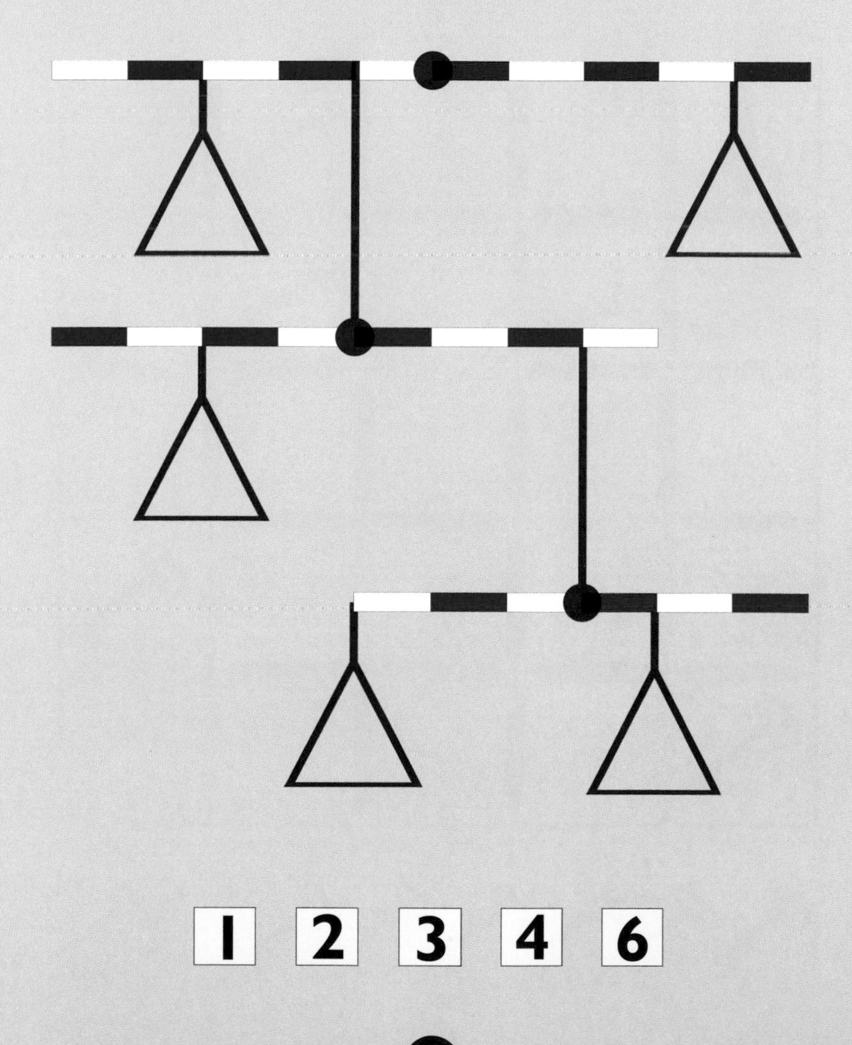

Help! I'm trapped in this jail and I need to get out. I've got nothing to escape with except for a couple of pieces of metal with which I could make two of the eight possible keys.

Which two keys should I choose to escape with, and what route should I take?

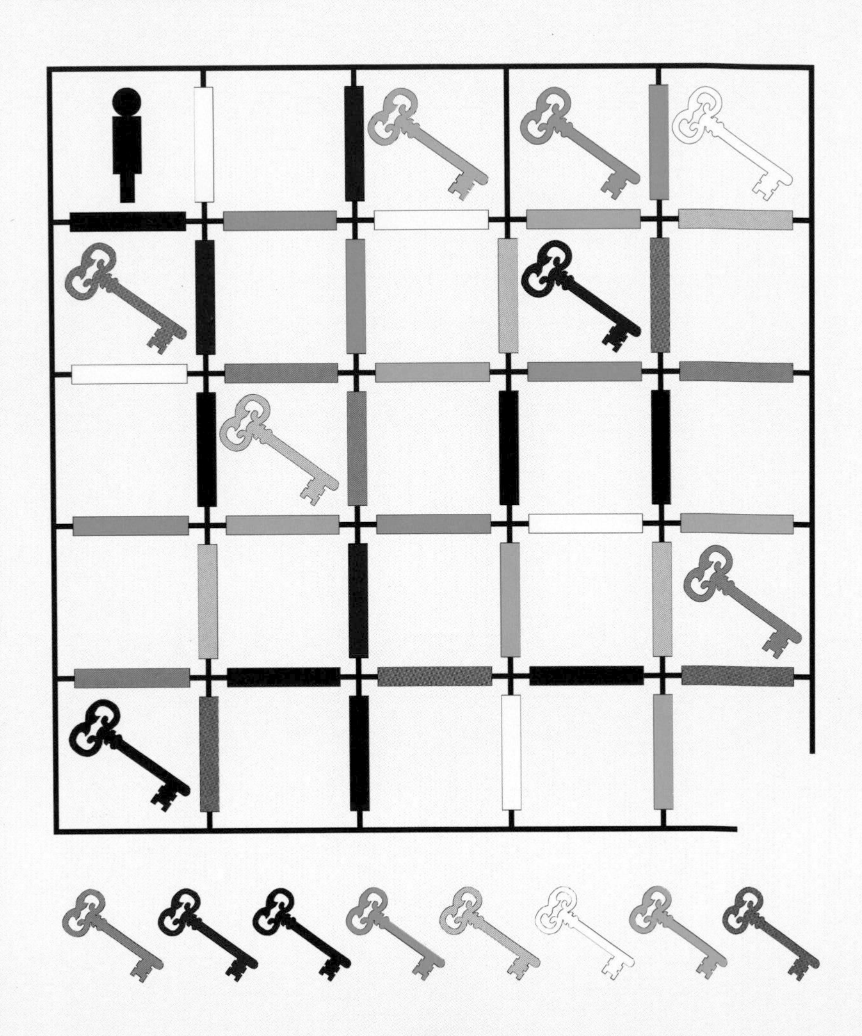

In this illusion, you need to cross your eyes. It will appear that the pictures are moving towards each other. When this starts to happen, don't look directly at the page or you will uncross your eyes again.

If you try hard enough, the two images will coalesce to form a three-dimensional crystal which appears to "glow".

You should see a three-dimensional crystal. If the crystal was real, how many edges would it have?

What's the longest word that can be read around this circle?

ANDROIDESERTSAROMATICKETSCISSORAN

What is the specific link between everything illustrated here?

DON'T INVERT THE BOOK YET. Look at the picture of this happy woman as printed for a few moments, then turn the page upside-down.

The result of that optical illusion should be self-evident. However, can you spot another mistake in the drawing?

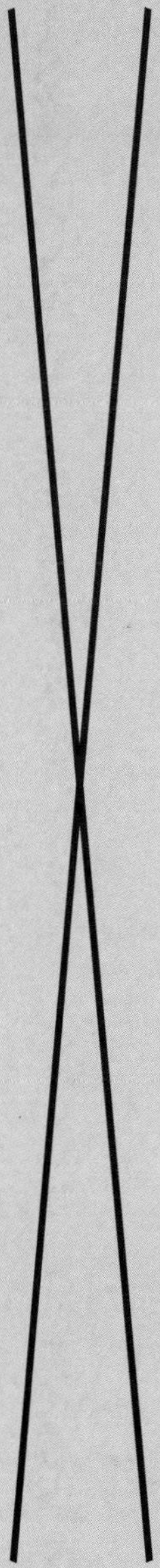

Time to make your own optical illusion!

The challenge here is to see if you can find a clear, optical illusion by looking at this basic pair of lines in a particular way.

Draw suitable boundaries on the page so that five related words are captured within those boundaries.

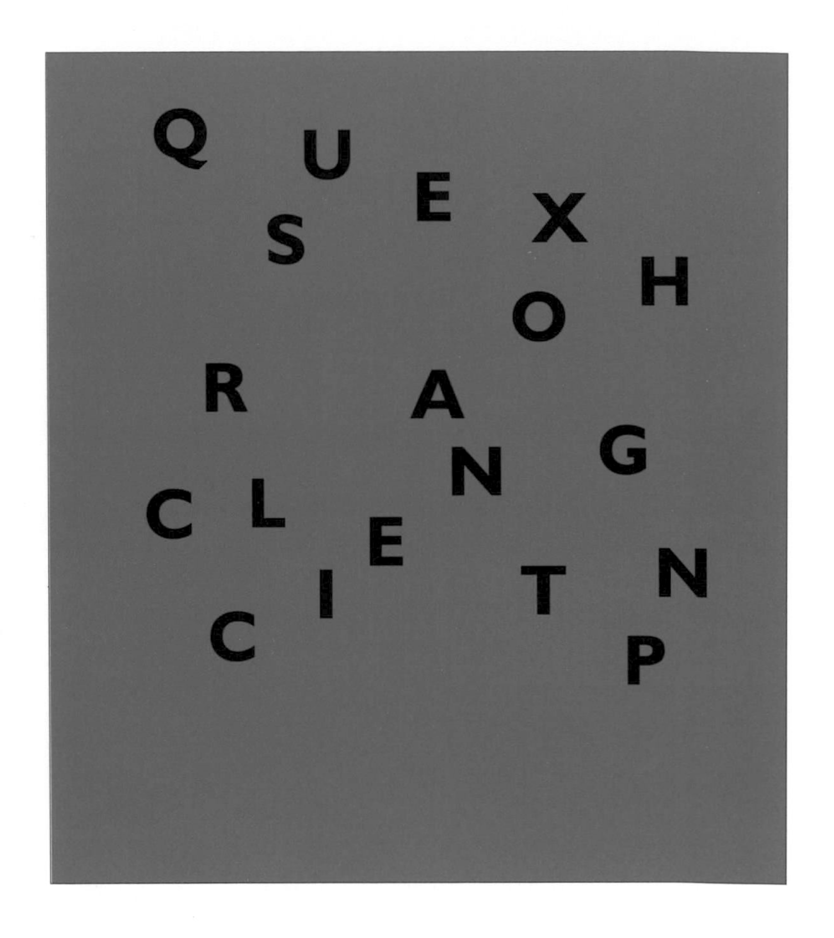

Fathom out the jigsaw, then answer the question that it poses.

I want to go home via any of the shortest routes available (in other words, always walking South or East). However, I also want to make sure I cross over exactly one bridge (in red).

How many different ways could I do this?

To solve this puzzle, you might like to consider at each intersection the number of ways there are of getting there via no bridges or one bridge (keeping the counts separate).

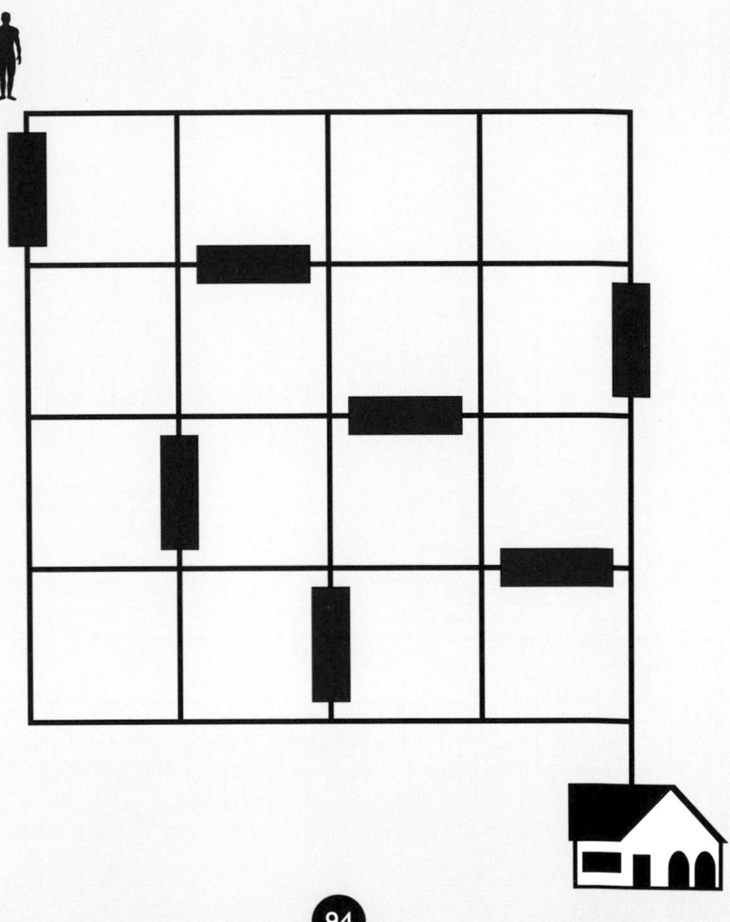

Here is a seemingly random pattern of lines and boxes. However, if you look carefully, your mind's eye should be able to work out a four-letter word.

What is that word?

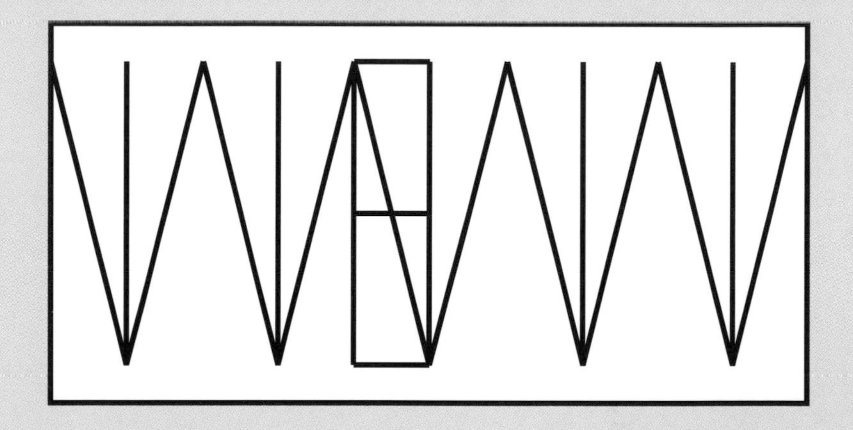

Look at the middle of this illusion. Do you see a square that isn't really there?

Connect up the four stars using four straight lines, none of which crosses a solid part of a circle, so that the end of the fourth line meets up with the beginning of the first.

I wasn't having a very good day at the pool hall. Hustler Henrietta had already taken pretty much all the folding money I had on me, and by now my pride was beginning to hurt.

By luck, I had managed to cover the final black with six of my yellow balls. Unfortunately, Henrietta made use of four cushions to pot the black and win.

Assuming that the angle at which a ball is rebounded is exactly equal to the angle makes with the cushion on its approach, how did she finish me off?

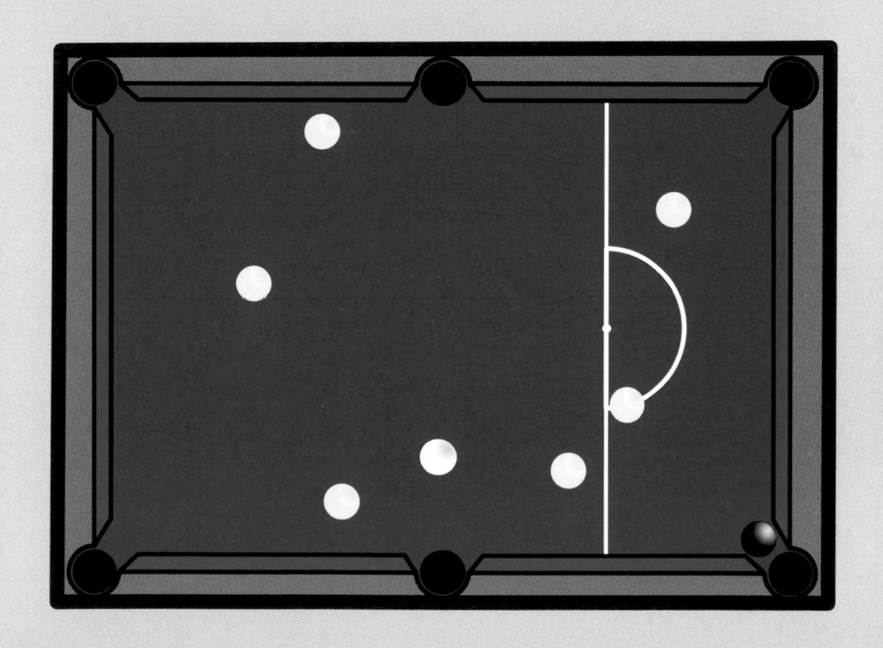

By rotating these three wheels, it is possible to align the segments so that you can draw a radial line (from the middle to the circumference) that only passes through areas of the same shade.

Of the five different shades, how many different shades is this feat possible *simultaneously*?

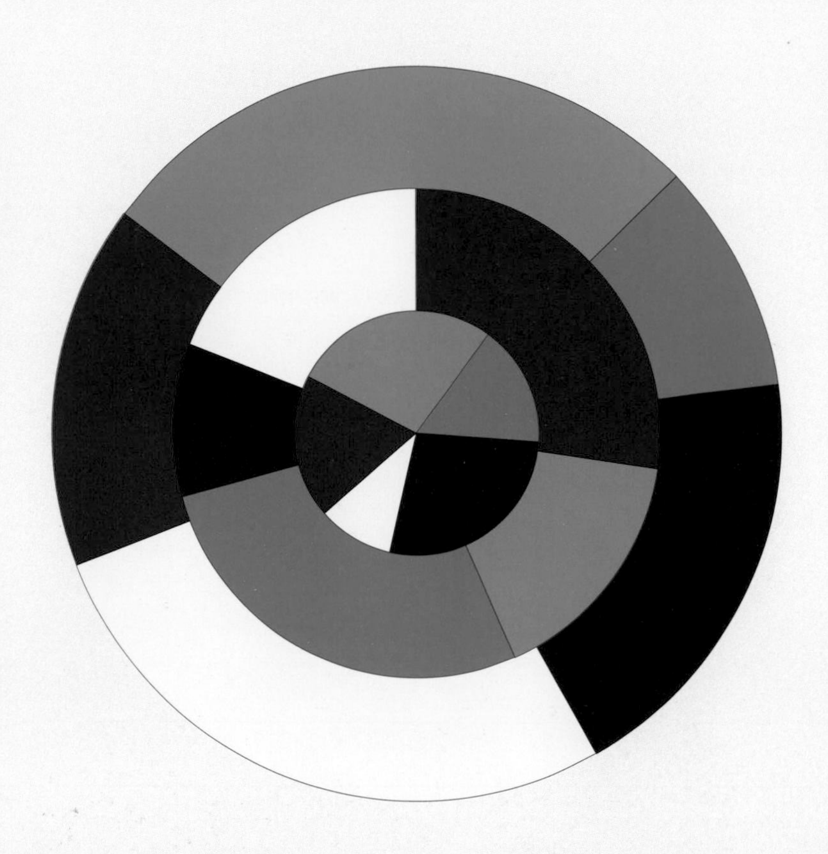

This puzzle uses an optical illusion called *size constancy*.

If you were looking at these sports balls, and they all *appear* as if they are the same size, then they must be at different distances away from you.

Place the balls in order, starting with those farthest away from you.

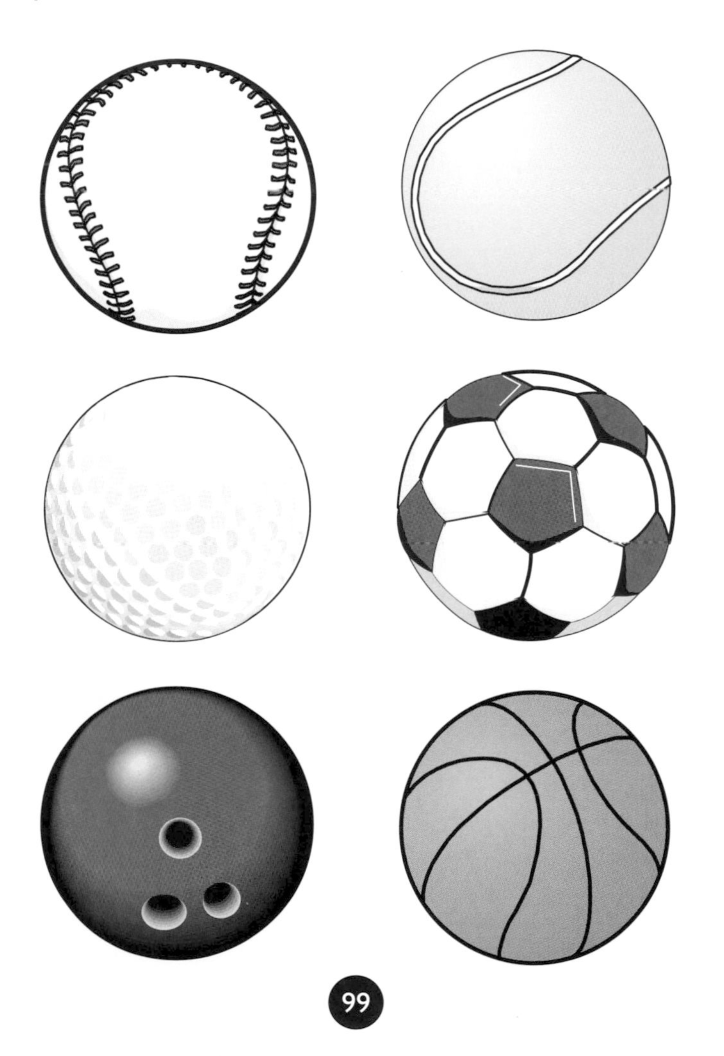

Ten of these objects are seen together,
The eleventh object is with them never.

Which is the odd one out?

ANSWERS

ANSWERS TO PUZZLES ENDING IN –1

1 Theoretically, there are eight possibilities (2 x 2 x 2), but only seven fit on the page:

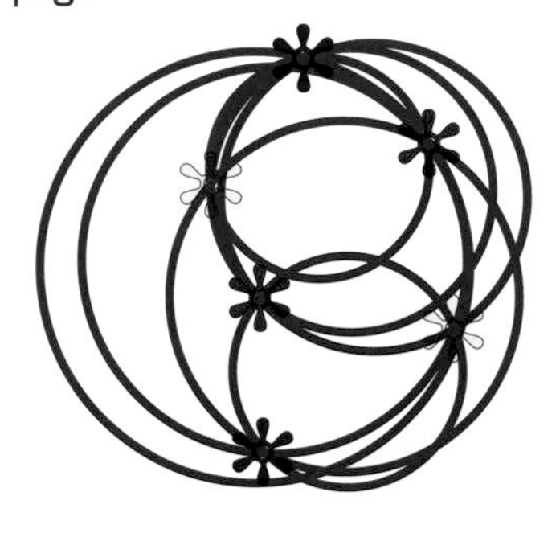

11 This arrangement has one large 4 x 4 square, four 3 x 3 ones, nine that are 2 x 2, and sixteen that are 1 x 1. Thirty in total.

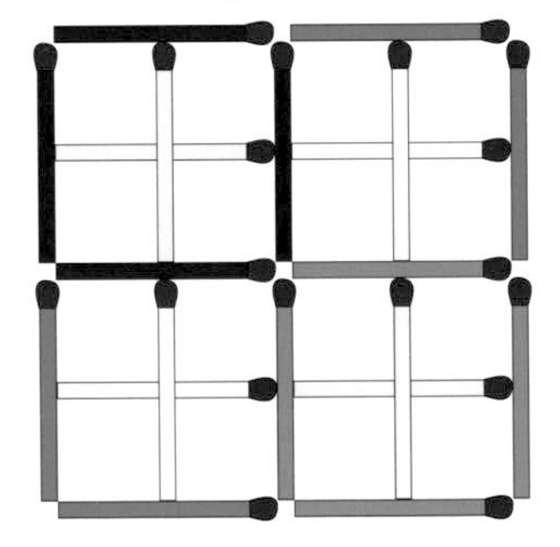

21 There is no letter L in the diagram.

31 "All good things must come to an end."

41 In this puzzle, you had a choice to make at several points. The correct route is as follows :

UP with the lark; RIGHT thinking; DOWN town (could have been UP); RIGHT wing (could have been LEFT); RIGHT as rain; UP the wall; RIGHT hook (could have been LEFT); UP draft (could have been DOWN); LEFT for dead; UP standing; LEFT winger (could have been RIGHT); LEFT behind; LEFT in the lurch; UP to tricks; RIGHT away; UP train; RIGHT side (could have been LEFT); RIGHT handed; RIGHT wrongs.

51

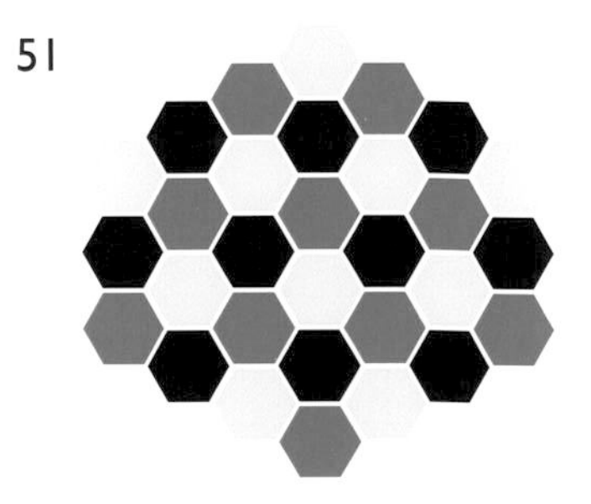

61 All the pictures were not what I asked for. I asked for a picture implying SCENT, but instead I have a picture of a CENT – similarly for WAIVE (wave), NOT (knot), TOO (two), RAIN (rein), OR (oar) and OUR (hour).

71

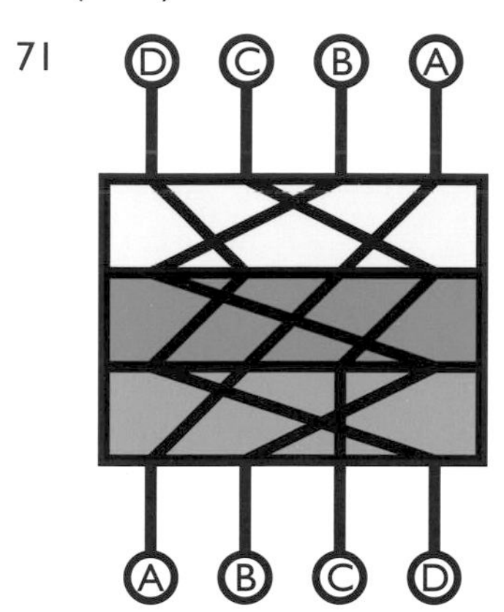

81

91 Hold the book so that it is almost vertical to your eyes. Additional lines should start appearing.

ANSWERS TO PUZZLES ENDING IN –2

2 The lettering of the pieces should have given the answer away!

12 This diagram proves that the yellow dot is half-way up the triangle, but the dark blue dot is at the center of gravity.

22 You will find the treasure in a CHEST:

32 Draw lines from each star to every other star. The numbers in the circles represent the number of lines that pass through them. Therefore, the white circle should have a "0" in it.

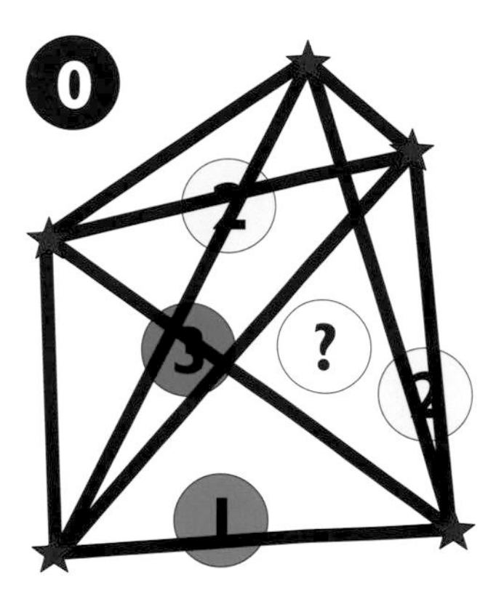

42 If you pair up CUP and POOL you phonetically get "couple", and similarly for BRA and ACE (brace) and TEA and WIN (twin). However, SING and GULL gives "single", and so is the odd one out.

52 Once all the lines have been connected up, shade in the areas which contain a black

dot. A simple picture of a duck will be formed.

62 The figure at the bottom-right is an ARC, not a circle.

72 There are 17 routes.

82 The prime factors of each number of teeth are:

$12 = \not{2} \times 2 \times 3$
$15 = \not{3} \times 5$
$16 = \not{2} \times 2 \times 2 \times 2$
$20 = 2 \times 2 \times 2 \times 5$
$22 = 2 \times 11$
$28 = \not{2} \times \not{2} \times 7$

Due to symmetry, some factors are crossed out (e.g. N looks the same upsidedown, and so looks like an N every 8 teeth.)

The lowest common multiple of the remaining numbers is:
$2 \times 2 \times 2 \times 3 \times 5 \times 7 \times 11$
$= 9240$. This is the smallest number which contains at least all the factors of each row (excluding the crossed-out ones).
As the entire system is turning at one tooth per second, 9240 corresponds to exactly 2 hours and 34 minutes.

92

ANSWERS TO PUZZLES ENDING IN –3

3 Stepping on a sequence of yellow-red-green spells the word HIJACKED.

13 Each triplet of stars mark the points of an equilateral triangle, except for the yellow star at the top:

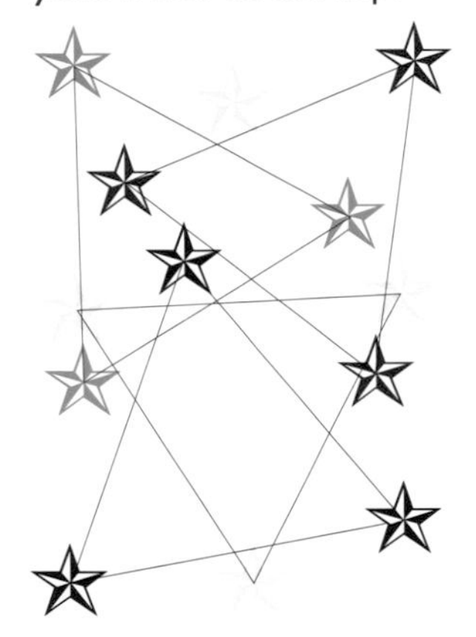

23 There are fifteen possible routes. This diagram shows the number of ways of getting to each point in the 4 x 4 grid:

1	1	1	1
3	2	1	2
3	8	10	2
3	3	13	15

33 The 17 large segments across the middle are easily counted. The number of smaller areas is 1 + 2 + 3 + 4 + 5 + 6 + 7 = 28 areas (try a situation with fewer circles to see why). So, the answer is:
17 + (2 x 28) = 73 areas.

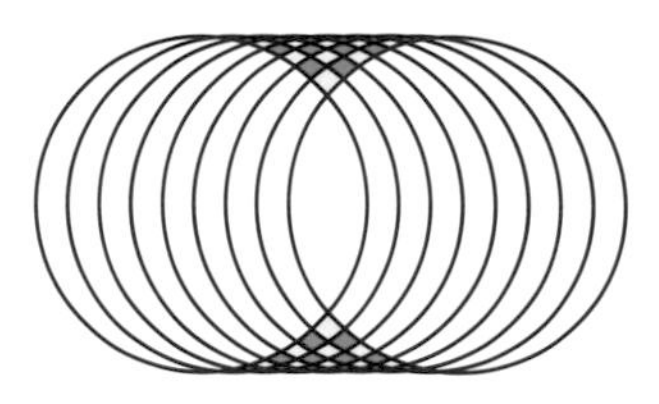

43 It is possible to trace all six diagrams.

53 All the words illustrated in the pictures (Radar, Zip code, Laser and Scuba) are in fact acronyms (RAdio Detection And Ranging, Zone Improvement Plan, Light Amplification by Stimulated Emission of Radiation, Self-Contained Underwater Breathing Apparatus).

63 If you took the key out of the lock, the points where

the pairs of pins meet would all line up. Therefore, the door could be opened without having any key at all. In fact, the door would only be secure if a key was left in the lock!

73

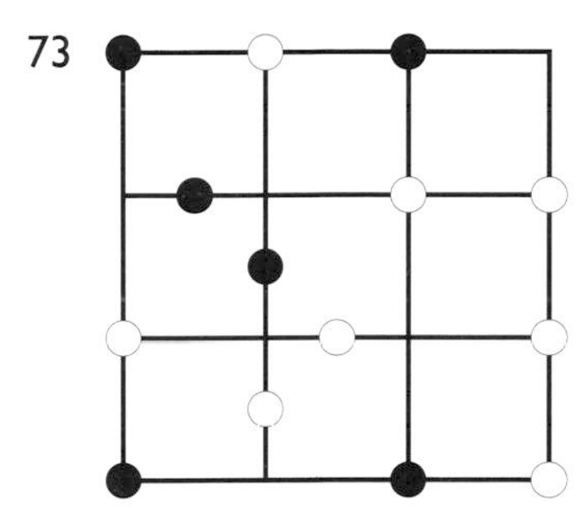

83 Suppose we started at one particular circle at the top, and ignore the sides of the hexagon for a moment. The number of different ways to get to any point is given by the famous Pascal's triangle:

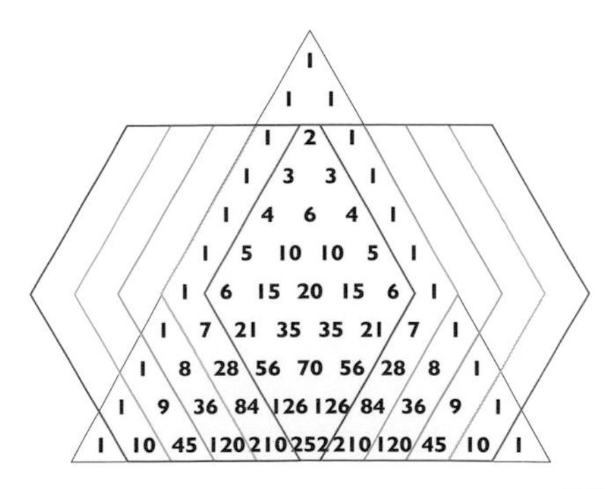

Note that the total of the bottom line is $1024 = 2^{10}$. By chopping off the appropriate parts of this diagram (where the sides of the hexagon would be), we can work out what the number of routes are for each of the five possible starting points on the top row (call these ABCDE). Starting at A or E means we can't use

((1+10+45+120+210)+1) x 2

routes. For B or D, this is

((1+10+45+120)+(10+1)) x 2

routes, and finally for C it is

(1+10+45)+(45+10+1).

So the final answer is:

(1024 x 5) – 774 – 374 – 112

= 3860 routes.

93 Reading the letters like a book, the message WHAT IS IN THE PICTURE is spelled out. The answer is "a rocking horse".

ANSWERS TO PUZZLES ENDING IN –4

4 Clue 2 says that the $1, $100 and $2 must be consecutive. As the $50 is in the dark blue space, this means the $100 must reside in either the black, pink, light blue or yellow space.

Now consider clues 1 and 3. If the $100 was in the black or yellow space (with the $1 and $2 either side), you would be left with three consecutive spaces remaining with the $5, $10 and $25 left to fill. This makes clues 1 and 3 impossible to satisfy.

Further investigation of the different cases shows that the $100 space cannot be pink, so it must be light blue. Hence, the only possible solution is: $1=Yellow, $2=Pink, $5=Red, $10=Black, $25=Green, $50=Dark blue, $100=Light blue.

14 The answer is A, because it is in black and the others are in different hues.
...Or is it E, because the others have left-right symmetry?
...Or is it I, because the others do not have serifs?
...Or is it O, because the rest are letters and O is a number?
...Or is it U, because it is the only shape that could be used as a container?

24 Z should be red. All the red letters can be written without taking your pen off the paper. All those in blue cannot.

34 The words spell: ONYX, OBOE, OXEN, ONTO, ORCA and OILY.

44 This is especially easy – it is possible to start and finish at almost any point you choose. The reason for this is that all of the intersections have an even number of routes leading out from them.

54 Each letter should be replaced by the number of “ends” which each letter has. For example, D is 0, M is 2, and T is 3. So, the answer to the final equation is $(4/2) + 3 - 4 = 1$. So the answer must be P (or possibly Q, depending on how you write it).

64 No matter what the exact numbers involved are, if X is even but Y is odd, the ball will end up in the blue pocket. If X is odd but Y is even, the ball goes into the yellow pocket. If both numbers are off, the ball will fall into the red pocket. Hence, the answers are blue, yellow, red.

74 None – it’s possible to get the ball out by continuously turning the maze clockwise.

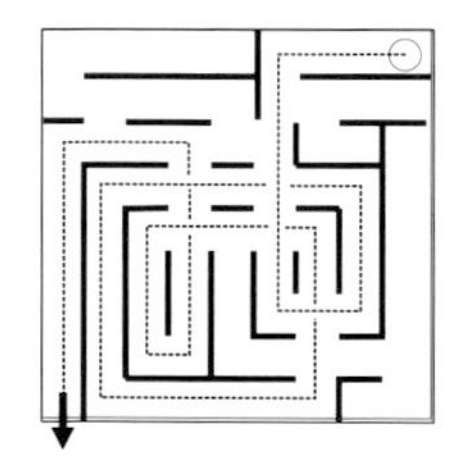

84

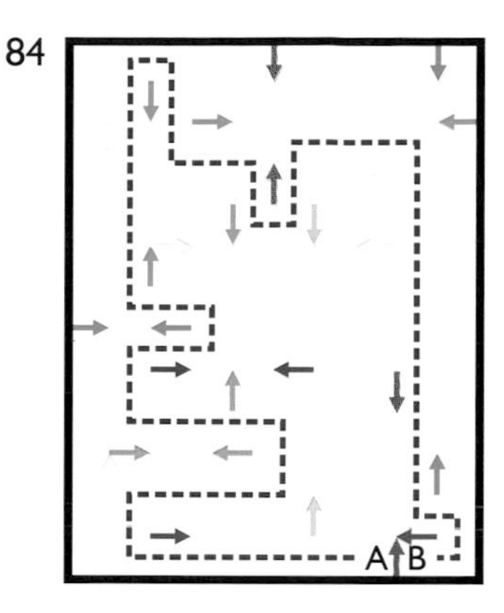

94 There would be 6 and 23 routes which include exactly no and one bridge respectively.

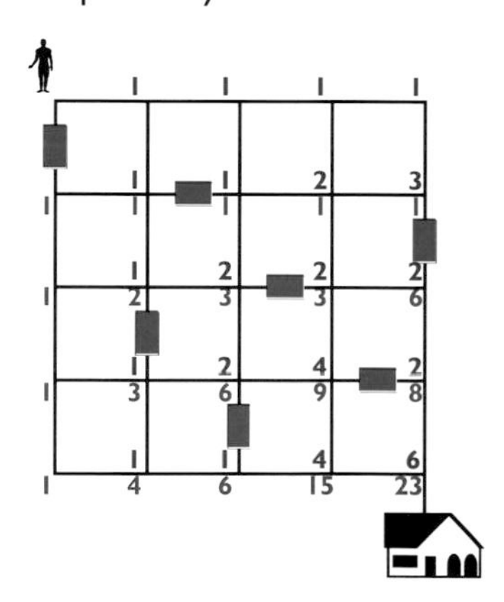

ANSWERS TO PUZZLES ENDING IN –5

5

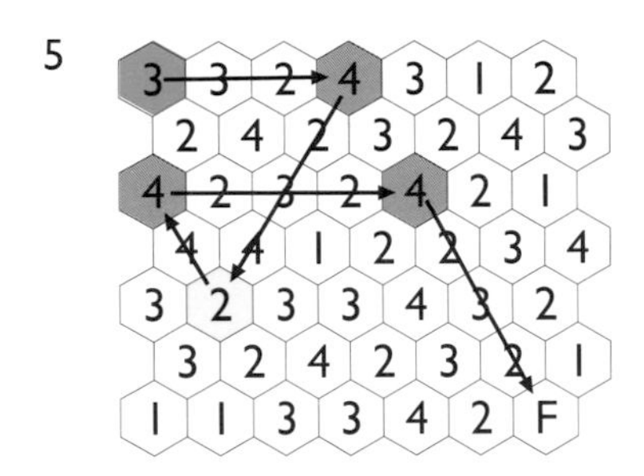

15 Perhaps surprisingly, the number of radial lines increases:

25 Symbol 3 would also appear as symbol 7. To form these shapes, the bottom-left quarter of each of the letters A to F have been reflected twice – once vertically, then horizontally.

35 The sequence moves in the direction illustrated. It starts with red, then red–orange, then red–orange–yellow, and so on building up the rainbow a little each time.

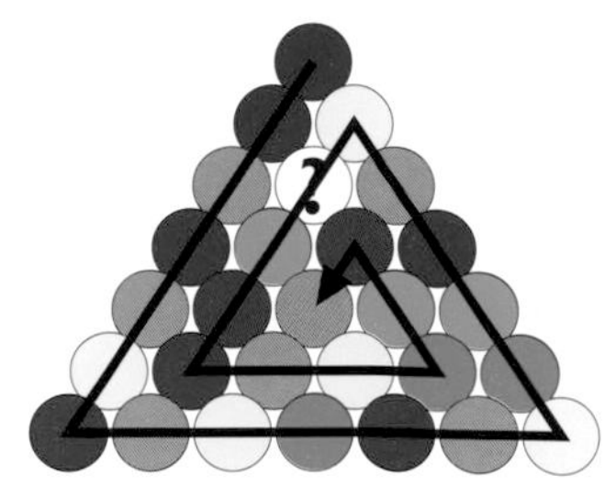

45 You need to use at least five yellow bricks, no matter which route you take. Of the remaining three yellow bricks left at your disposal, you have free choice of going along any of the five yellow columns. This is the same as putting three balls into any of five bags.
If we consider this equivalent problem, there are 5 ways of putting all three into one bag,
5 x 4 ways of putting two into one bag and one into another bag, and
(5 x 4) / 2 ways of putting

the balls into three separate bags. The answer is therefore:
5 + 20 + 10 = 35 ways (for either version of the puzzle).

65

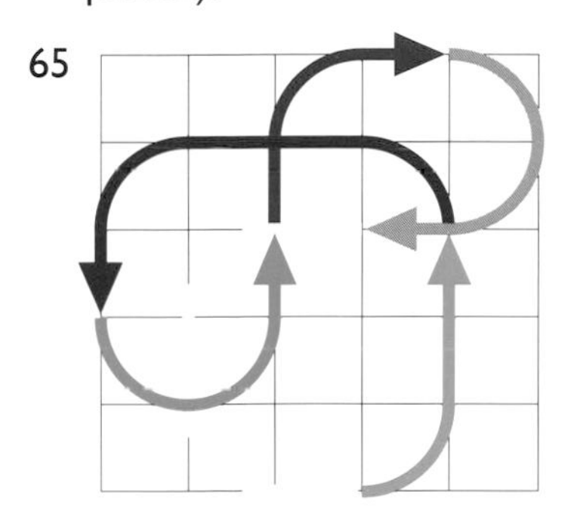

75 Across: Lager, Oats, Creme, Nut, Bran. Down: Lemon, Tart, Egg, Bean, Sauce.

85 Top row: 2 and 4,
Middle row: 6,
Bottom row: 1 and 3.

95 The word VIEW can be seen.

ANSWERS TO PUZZLES ENDING IN –6

6 It's possible to do it by removing just three lines:

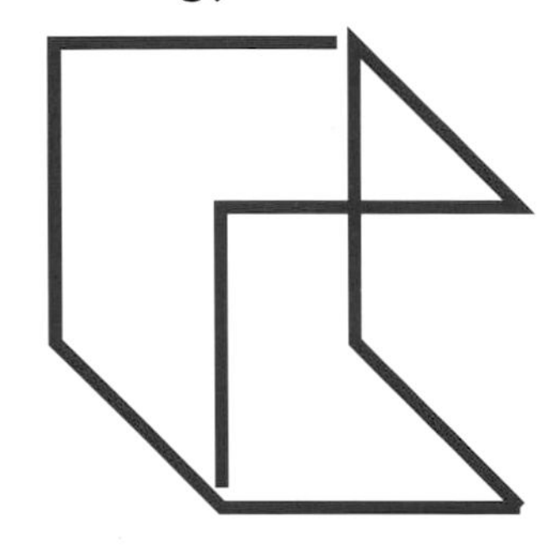

16 The letters given here refer to compass directions taken at each junction:

1) E, N, S (yes)
2) E, N, W, N (yes)
3) E, N, W, S, N (no)
4) E, N, W, S, W (no)
5) E, S, E, N (yes)
6) E, S, E, W, N (no)
7) E, S, E, W, S (yes)
8) E, S, W (no)
9) S, E, N (yes)
10) S, E, W, N, S (no)
11) S, E, W, N, W (no)
12) S, E, W, S (yes)
13) S, N, N, S (yes)
14) S, N, N, W, N (yes)
15) S, N, N, W, S (no)
16) S, N, W (no)

The probability of choosing route 1 and 9 is 1/8 (because those routes involve three 50-50 choices). The probability for routes 2, 5, 12 and 13 is 1/16, and for routes 7 and 14 it is 1/32. Adding these together gives the answer 9/16.

26 Do you see a triangle that doesn't exist here?

36 Dali, da Vinci and van Gogh were artists. To my knowledge, Abraham Lincoln was not.

46 Each word represents the change in its background. TRAFFIC goes from green to yellow to red, like a traffic light. LITMUS goes from red to blue, like litmus paper. SUNBURN goes from pink to brown to red, like sunburnt skin. So what goes from green to yellow to brown to black? A banana!

56 Ignore the spare coin! Instead, move one coin from the left pile to the right. Remembering that each pan weighs one coin also, we now have 8 coins weight at 3 spaces from the pivot on the left, and 6 coins weight at 4 units from the pivot.
8 x 3 = 24 = 6 x 4, hence balances.

66 It is the letters of INCOGNITO merged together.

76 *Brief Encounter*, *Home Alone* (Home and "a loan"), *The Magnificent Seven* (magnify-cent 7), *Terminator*, *The King and I*, *West Side Story*.

86

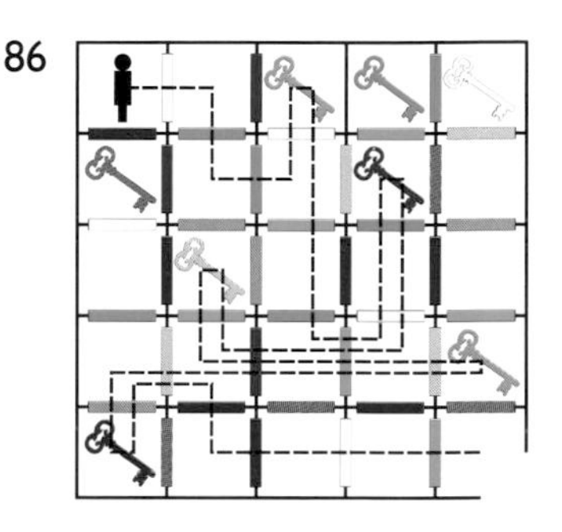

96

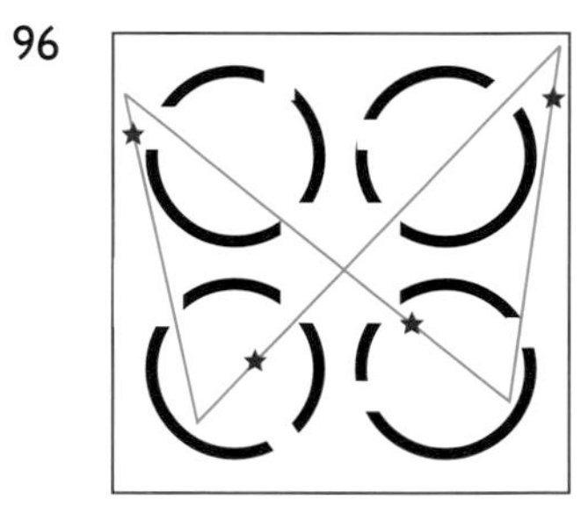

ANSWERS TO PUZZLES ENDING IN –7

7 The top nail will catch the rope. Here, we have joined the two ends together and shaded the regions that are on the inside of the resulting loop:

17 When the rocket is complete, the word DISCOVERY is spelled out:

27

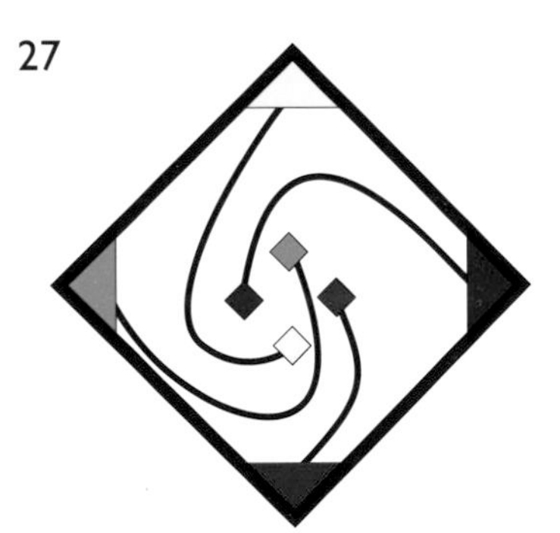

It is always possible to do this, regardless of the arrangement of the diamonds.

37

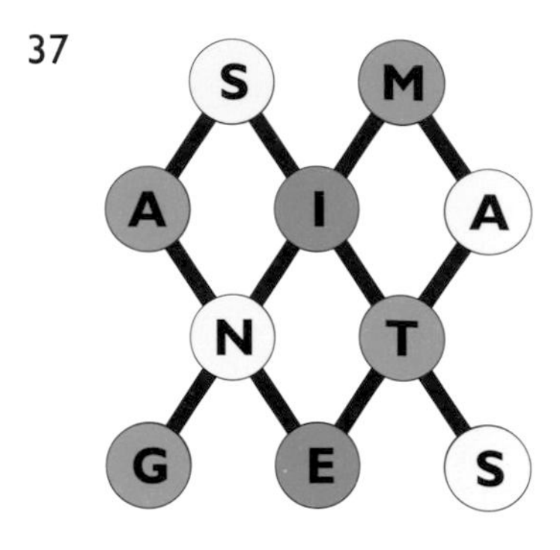

47 "Where you have a choice of only left or right at T-junctions, always turn left."

57 The correct route is illustrated here in red:

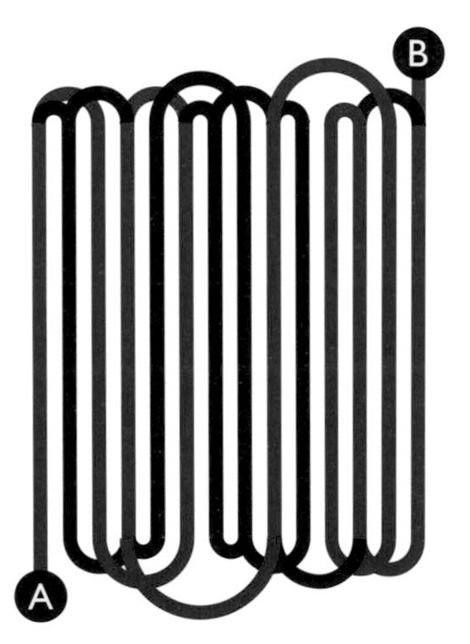

67 On each row, we have 44, 44 and "forty-four"!

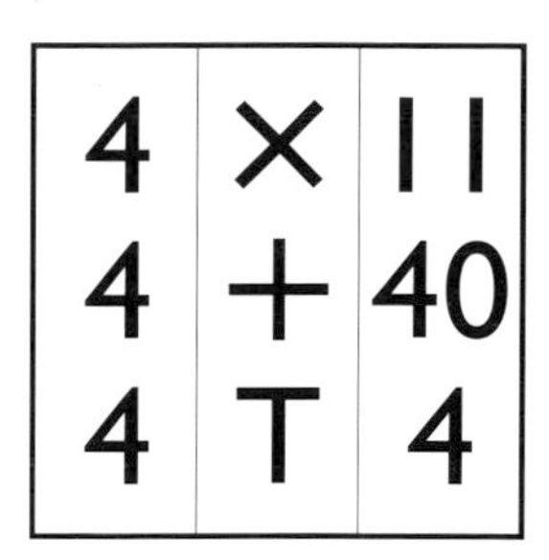

77 The correct route is 164134734674, which totals 50.

87 There would be 52 edges.

97

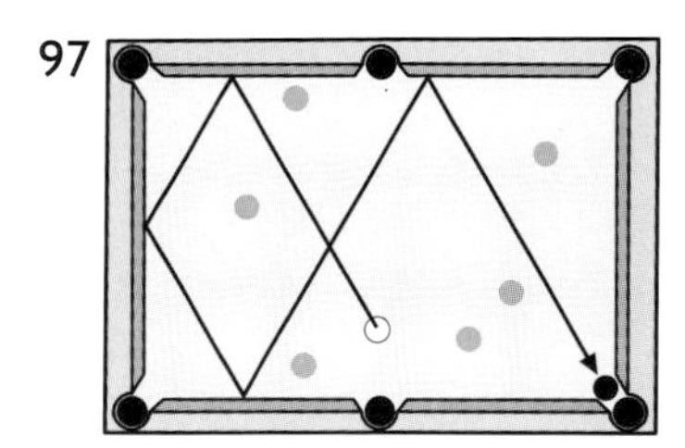

ANSWERS TO PUZZLES ENDING IN –8

8 Shading the targets demonstrates that there are seventeen different targets:

18 If you correctly identified all the places bets could be made, you'd make a cool profit of $163:

Type of bet	*Bets*	*Odds*	*Win*
Black	1	Evens	$1
Odd	1	Evens	$1
Range 1-18	1	Evens	$1
2nd column	1	2-1	$2
Range 13-24	1	2-1	$2
Line of 6 (A)	2	5-1	$10
Square of 4 (B)	4	8-1	$32
Line of 3 (C)	1	11-1	$11
Pair (D)	4	17-1	$68
Single (E)	1	35-1	$35
		TOTAL	***$163***

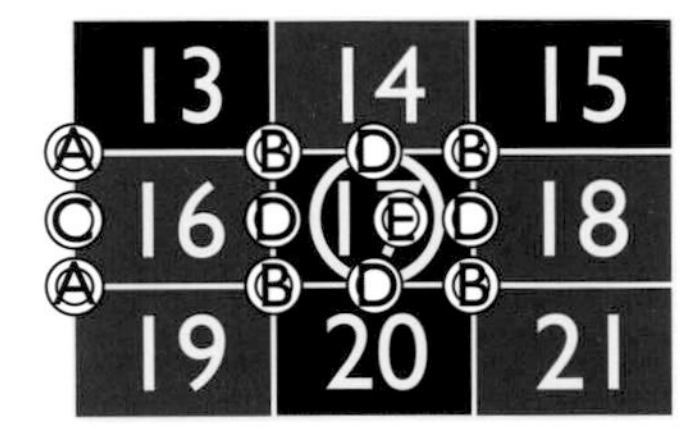

28 A chair and a gunman both have ARMS; a potato and a needle both have EYES; you can have a HEAD of water and a head of hair; a clock has HANDS and bananas come in bunches called "hands".

38 The staircase was a bit of a hint: you needed to turn the 6 and 9 upside-down to get this to work:

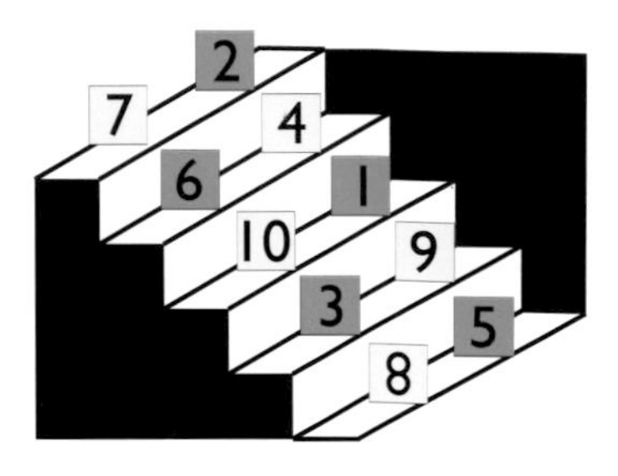

48 Six moves are required.

58

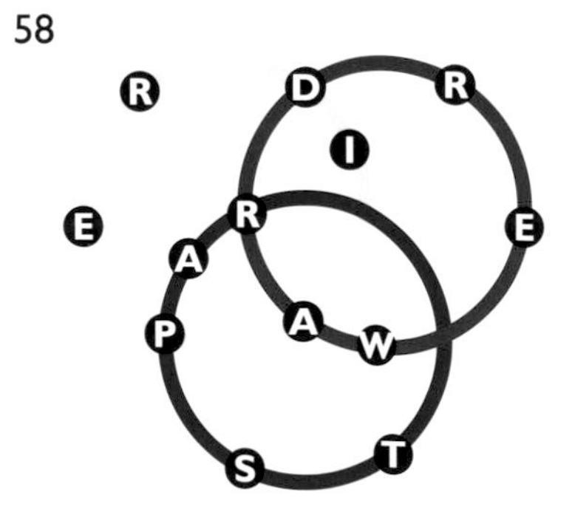

68 If you assume top-right is TRUE, then squares on middle row (blue and orange) are FALSE and the rest are true. However, if you assume top-right is FALSE, you just get the opposite result. Hence, you can't tell anything.

78

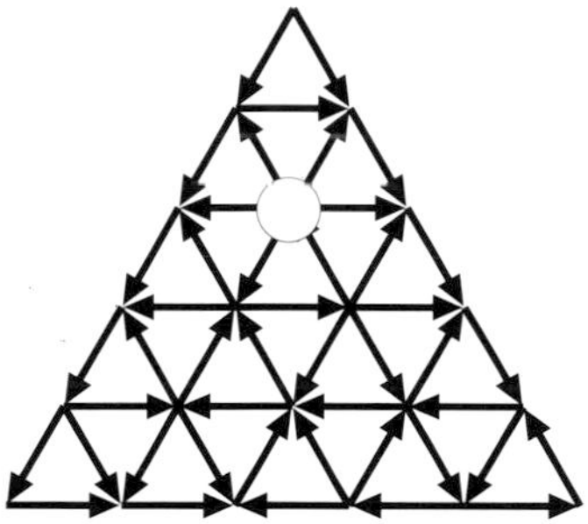

88 Starting from near the 10 o'clock position of the circle, the word DISTRACTION can be read in the red letters.

98 It is possible to arrange the wheels so that the feat can be performed for all five shades at once:

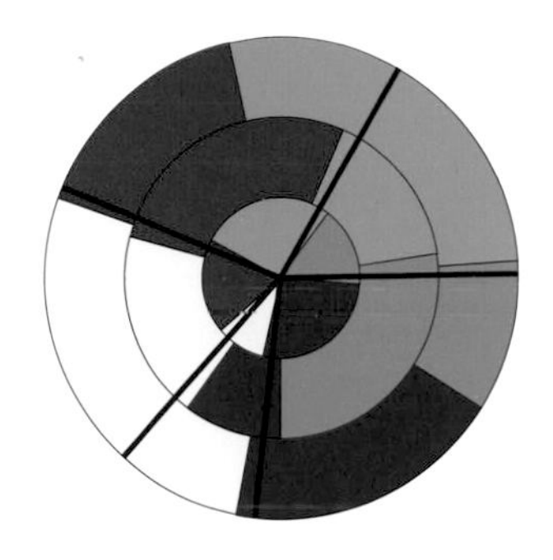

ANSWERS TO PUZZLES ENDING IN –9

9 Perhaps surprisingly, the cube will still have the blue face uppermost. This is why the geometry of the figure looks so convincing, despite it being impossible to construct physically.

19 It appears that the "O" should be a "W". However, this is a French compass, and West is "Ouest" in French. (The other letters remain the same: North = Nord; South = Sud; East = Est).

29 Adjusting each wheel a few degrees makes the word LEXICOGRAPHER appear:

39 The combination was 45. The false statements were A (it was Paul McCartney and *Wings*), F (it is Rabat), I (it is part of a castle), K (it is drawn by Jim Davis), and M (Straw-weight is the lightest).

49 Turning four of the circles forms the illusion of a cube:

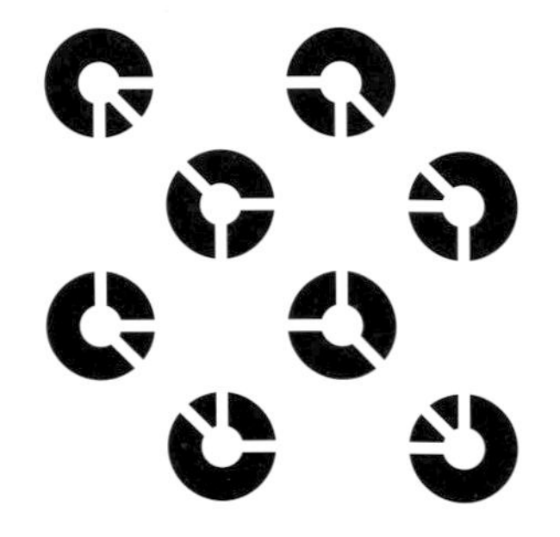

59

69 Three – the first, third and sixth need to be inverted, as you may have guessed by looking at the stars.

79 All those items come in, or are usually used in, pairs.

89 They are all eponyms (named after people).

99 Basket ball, soccer ball, bowling ball, base ball, tennis ball, golf ball.

ANSWERS TO PUZZLES ENDING IN –0

10 If the blue line is 100 units long, then the red line is 100 cos 45° = 70.7 units long. Hence, the first 70 circles will not be cut by the square.

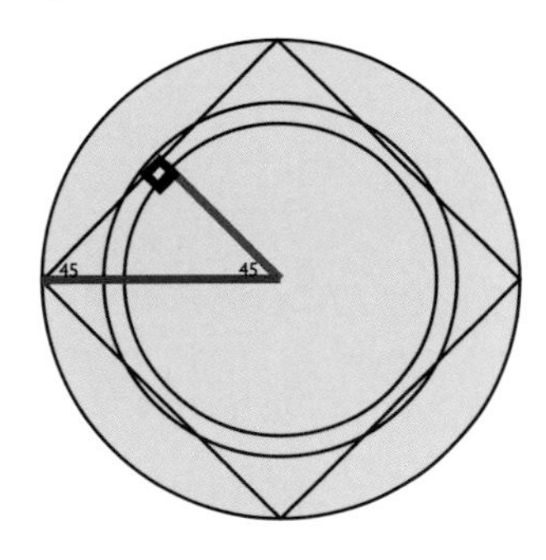

20 Given clues 1 and 3, the black ring must be top-middle or top-right. No matter what combination you try, black will not work in the top-right (the fact that yellow cannot link with red or green always gets in the way).

So black must be top-middle. You then have to try up to two further times to see if blue goes in the top-left or top-right (only the former situation works), leading to this solution:

30

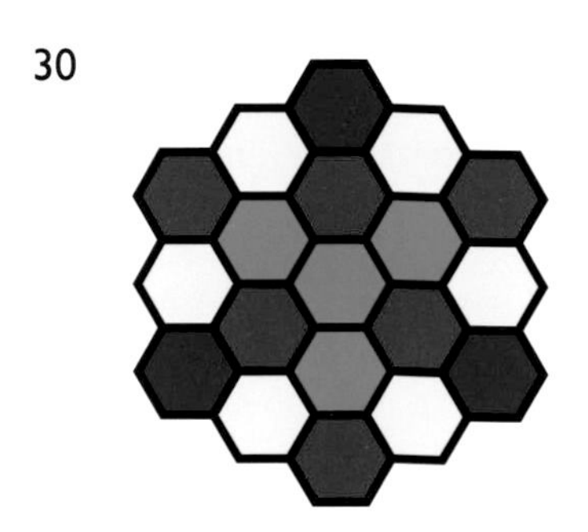

40 The towns are Cherbourg, Chantilly, Cannes, Cognac, Chablis and Calais.

50

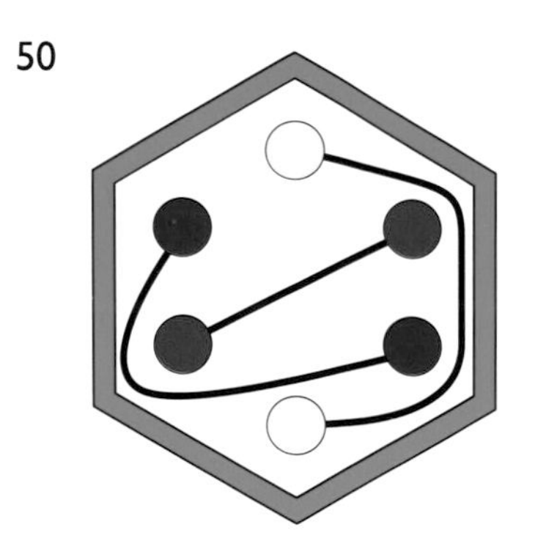

60 The word is DART, appropriately enough.

70 Absolutely none – just go around the back of the coat hanger where you can read the word AUTOMATA.

80 Turn the page on its side to see the letters K, E, H and D.

90 Her eyes are also upside-down.

100 The motorbike – the others are the tokens in a traditional set of Monopoly.